THE EAGLE THAT DRANK HUMMINGBIRD NECTAR

A Novel About
Personal Transformation
In Business Leaders

by
Aneace Haddad

Access Your Surprise Gift

Thank you so much for purchasing my book. To show my appreciation, I've prepared a special gift for you with lots of exercises and other exclusive content related to my book. Access it by visiting www.aneace.com/nectar

Table Of Contents

Part One
Entering the Path

Hearing the Call

Last night, I dreamt of an eagle under a pile of wet leaves, suffering from the apathy of a midlife crisis — I knew this the way we know things in dreams. Or maybe he was trying to die, I couldn't tell.

Obviously, dreams aren't premonitions, but I wanted to share my dream with Matt because I was sure he would see it as a sign that at least one of the eagles in the rainforest was still alive. He was convinced he had seen the eagle two days ago, on one of our walks through the jungle, but his mother, Misha, said it was just his imagination. Maybe the eagle really was recovering somewhere. Even if dreams aren't omens, at least Matt would know that one of the few men in his life believed him.

I showered, got dressed, and ran down the two flights of stairs to Misha's apartment, hoping to catch Matt before he left for school.

Misha and Matt were in the kitchen having breakfast.

"This is early, even for you," Misha said. "Is everything OK? Any news from your daughter?"

"None."

It was three weeks since my fiftieth birthday, and Val still hadn't called from wherever she was in Samoa.

Misha turned to Matt. "Aidan is here. Say good morning."

Matt stared at his phone, ignoring his mother.

"Yo! Matt!"

"Mmm." He didn't lift his eyes from his phone.

"And finish your breakfast!"

"It's funny how your accent changes," I said, "especially when you raise your voice."

"Yeah?"

"Usually it's kind of British..."

"Scottish."

"... but when you just said Yo! Matt, you sounded almost American."

She shrugged. I wondered if she ever took on an Indian accent.

"So Matt," I said, "I dreamt about the eagle."

Misha squinted at me.

"Was it dead?" Matt looked at me while holding his cereal spoon in front of his mouth.

"No... alive."

"Yes!" Matt pumped his fist.

"Look, I know it was just a dream, but it felt real."

"I'm sure I saw him the other day!"

"I believe you."

I glanced at Misha. Sure enough, she was squinting at me. I knew what she was thinking... I shouldn't get Matt's hopes up.

"What was your dream?" Matt's bowl was at least half full.

"I was standing in a garden, holding a rake, staring at a pile of wet leaves where an animal was hiding. I thought it was a rat, a big one."

"Yuck."

"Yeah... pretty gross. I turned the rake around and used the wooden end to poke at the leaves."

"Did the rat attack you?"

"A large bird popped its head out, glaring at me. It was an

eagle... THE eagle. His feathers were wet and discoloured, like a human body left too long in water, all faded and pale."

"Aidan!" Misha wrinkled her nose. "We're having breakfast!"

Matt laughed.

"I touched it again with the rake, hoping to get the eagle to move into the sunshine. So it could dry off and recover."

There was more to the dream, or there was another dream, which seemed important too... but that second part was already distant.

"Was it OK?"

I wasn't sure what to say at this point. For some reason, it felt like the eagle had given up on life and wanted to be left to die under the wet leaves. I could still see the eagle glaring at me. I was an intruder, disturbing its dying process. But it wasn't dead, that was the crucial bit. There was still hope.

"It eventually climbed out of the leaves and dried itself in the sun," I lied. "Then flew away."

The dream didn't have that bit at all.

"Good morning, Mister Perez," Misha's helper walked past us carrying Matt's backpack with his school things.

"Good morning, Gloria."

She set the backpack down at the door then started to gather up the breakfast dishes, leaving Matt with his bowl.

"I discovered why certain foods change our moods," Matt said. "It's all about evolution."

This would be a long story; I could tell by the cheerful sound of his voice. This was good.

"Bacteria in our gut transforms food into energy and mood chemicals like serotonin. Trillions of bacteria. All connected through a kind of internet... a gut brain. It's called the... hold on," he looked at his tablet, "... the enteric nervous system. And different foods create different mood chemicals. I don't know why evolution did that. I still have to figure that out."

"That's cool!"

Misha was smiling now, proud. Matt could study anything he wanted and would excel.

"Wanna hear something really cool? Researchers are trying

to create a super intelligent bacteria-powered fuel cell. Just like the gut. Imagine robots that get their energy from eating! Do you think that would give them feelings and emotions too, like the bacteria in our guts?"

"I... I don't know."

"I want to be a robotics engineer. What kind of biology would I need to study?"

"Well, you'd need to study computer science and robotics."

"Yeah, but people who create bacteria-powered fuel cells... they must have studied some kind of biology too."

"Microbiology? Neuroscience?"

He nodded, then stared at his tablet while walking back to his room.

"I'm going to build a robotic animal. Maybe a horse. Or a mule, that would be better, a mule can carry stuff."

Whenever he let his imagination roam wild, everything else fell in place. His mind needed the stimulation.

"You need to be out the door in five minutes," Misha said.

"I know!"

After Matt left, Misha turned to me.

"When I told you not to discourage him from believing the eagle was alive, I didn't mean for you to get his hopes up."

"Yeah, I hope..."

"You hope? You hope what?"

I shook my head.

"Actually, you know what I think about your dream?"

I stared at her, not sure if I wanted to hear.

"I think it says more about what you're going through."

"Me?"

"You can't see it?" She glared at me. "The eagle rotting under wet leaves? Like it had given up? You still can't see?"

"I guess that's how you see me."

"The vision is so appropriate... languishing under wet leaves, wasting away. That's how you're feeling. You've said so yourself!"

"I'm doing things. I'm mentoring a bunch of startups, I'm coaching people..."

"Look, Aidan, you know me. I care about you. Matt cares

about you. We both love you. You're a wonderful friend." She reached out and touched my hand. "But I'm worried about you."

"I'm..."

"You're languishing. Other people might not see it. But I do. On the outside you're this very successful and confident man who sold his tech company..."

"I didn't get much money out of it..."

"... but they don't see..." Misha froze, then got up to put the milk away.

"What? They don't see what?"

"You don't laugh like you used to. You're not passionate about your work. I don't know what you're excited about anymore."

What she was saying wasn't entirely false.

"I... don't know why I'm in Singapore anymore. Now that Val is gone..."

She nodded.

"You'll hear from her soon. I'm sure she's fine."

"Yeah..."

I scrolled through the pictures on my phone, and pulled up Val's last message, a video from a month ago. There she was, on my screen, in the palm of my hand, just as young and bubbly and beautiful as ever. Misha squeezed in closer to me so she could watch. I pressed play.

"Papa, you're probably sleeping right now," Val leaned in toward the phone and spoke in her slightly French accent. "It's very early in Singapore, so I'm leaving you this message, instead of calling. I'm going to help on the other side of the island, and probably won't have internet for a while. I'm well. I feel useful and needed. Don't worry about me." She looked away, briefly, as if someone was waiting for her. "Your birthday is coming soon. I wish I was with you this year. It's the first year we don't celebrate a birthday together!" She hesitated again, looking very thoughtful, in that pained way that always made me wonder if I had said something that hurt her.

I pressed pause on the video.

"Wait," Misha said, "don't turn it off. You always pause halfway!"

"That was pretty much it. I need to get going."

I stood up to leave.

"Aidan... I'd be freaking out too if I didn't hear from my child for so long." Misha hugged me. Then she stepped back and gave me that look that said she was going me some advice. "But it's not just Singapore."

"What?"

"You said you don't know why you're still here..."

"Now that Val is gone."

"She's an adult."

"Exactly." I wanted to add that Matt was sixteen and was still living at home, so Misha didn't know what it was like.

"Here's what I think," she continued, "you don't know who you are anymore. The Aidan you used to be is languishing. And you haven't decided who you want to be next."

I wanted to argue with her, but I knew she was right. The dream vision of decay matched my life. It described my situation in a visceral and profound way. I still had cash from the sale, and I didn't have any obligations anymore, with Val grown and independent. I didn't have to travel, and I had lots of time to explore what I wanted to do next. I should have been excited about all the opportunities I could pursue next. Instead, I was overwhelmed by a sense of emptiness and dread, reflected perfectly in my dream.

"Sometimes," I said, "it's easier to find purpose when your back is up against the wall, and you just have to make things happen."

"Is that what you're waiting for?"

I shrugged.

"Seems to me you've been up against a wall for a while already."

Back in my apartment, I sat down on the sofa and looked at Val's video again. I started it at the middle.

"I feel useful and needed. Don't worry about me," she said. "Your birthday is coming soon. I wish I was with you this year. It's the first year we don't celebrate a birthday together!"

I pressed pause, so I could look closely at her eyes. Yes, there was pain. She was probably worried about me. I pressed play again.

"Papa, there is something I have wanted to tell you. These last four years with you have been wonderful. I'm so glad I convinced you to come with me to Singapore. I will always cherish the time we had together. And... if you're still worried about being away when I was growing up, please stop. You have more than made up for that." She laughed, and then became serious. "And Papa, please remember this... and I hope you hear this... really hear this... the accident would have happened anyway. Even if the car worked perfectly. It wasn't your fault." Then her face became light and smiley again. "Now... I hope the next time we speak; you've found a girlfriend.... finally... and maybe you'll have plans about starting another tech company! J't'aime mon p'tit Papa!"

The video froze, ending on her big smile.

Comforting me shouldn't be her responsibility. She's my daughter, I'm the adult. At the same time though... it did feel good.

Refusing the Call

Dreams, when they're powerful, have a way of colouring everything happening in our lives. Like a background landscape of moods or emotions — a dreamscape. They are a glimpse into the subconscious mind, which is probably even more amazing and magical than a premonition. If premonitions show you a possible future, often outside of your control, dreams show how you're creating the future, often subconsciously. That's what made this dream even more frightening.

The image of the rotting eagle stayed with me throughout the day. It was such a disturbing memory that I didn't immediately realize there was a second part to the dream. That would come to me that evening, at an event I was co-facilitating with Misha at Singapore's newest, ultra-modern triple towers, called Marina Bay Sands.

"This city is so rich," Misha said, while taking in the evening view from the iconic Skypark straddling the tops of three towers, fifty-seven levels above ground. "That's why I love doing business here."

A string quartet played classical music on a platform behind us, the musician's silhouettes standing out with the evening sky behind them.

"So, how have I done?" I wanted her feedback, hopeful she could give me more work.

She glanced over her shoulder at a group of startup founders in their twenties and thirties, letting off steam after delivering their pitches at one of South-East Asia's more prestigious investor competitions. When I looked over at them, they raised their glasses to me with big smiles.

"They like you, Aidan," she said.

"I've been in their shoes."

"You're a good mentor. Their presentations were a lot better tonight. Let's see how many are able to attract investors after the gala."

"They'll find investors. I'm sure of it."

I turned back toward the group of founders holding their drinks, getting louder as the evening wore on and their excitement grew. A young man raised his glass and nodded his head at me, with a big smile. He walked over to us.

"We nailed it," he said, lowering his voice but still sounding very excited about his presentation to the panel of judges.

"You did well," said Misha.

"So, what, who cares, why me," he said, "that's just so simple and brilliant."

He was referring to the framework I had developed for start-up investor pitches. So what? Why in the world is your project important? Who cares? Who benefits the most from your project? Why me? What is your personal engagement? Why is the project so special to you? Every team I worked with needed to answer these three questions with few words and lots of emotion, so that investors could connect viscerally with the startup. It was a process I had used for years to attract employees, customers, and investors.

As I looked at the founders standing around joking with their peers from other companies, I felt proud. I had watched many of them struggle and grow as I challenged their startup stories. Initially, almost every one of them was focused entirely on spreadsheets and financials, because that's what they thought was expected. Many of them found it difficult to step back and create a deeply personal pitch, sharing something meaningful from their past, maybe even from childhood, that drove home why their project was so important to them. They weren't used to showing the vulnerability needed to be authentic. But eventually, almost all of them managed to make their pitches real and vulnerable.

It was amazing to watch the transformation. It was as if they suddenly gave themselves permission to be both analytical and personal. In a way, they became more human. A sense of deep satisfaction and confidence would appear, that always reminded me of how I often felt after a deep meditation session. They were there to win the competition, definitely. But in my opinion, when that transformation happened, they had already won.

When I looked at Misha, I noticed she had been staring at me with a little smirk.

"What?"

She shook her head, and the smirk grew.

"What," I said, "tell me."

"You're teaching," she said. "You know that, right? You're not really coaching."

This had become her pet subject. The thing I did best, was apparently something I wasn't supposed to do.

"Look," she said, "There's nothing wrong with teaching. When you're teaching, teach... but when you're coaching, coach. Don't mix them up, until you've mastered them separately. Right now, you tend to mix them up."

I looked away, avoiding eye contact. She leaned in toward me, forcing me to look at her.

"You're very good at what you do," she said. "You connect very well with people. They respect you. They learn from you. But you're cruising on charisma and your successful founder aura."

"That seems to be enough with this group."

She nodded.

"Yes, it is. But I'll run out of work for you if you don't get serious about coaching. You have real talent. I'm afraid you're wasting it."

"I need another drink," I said, "can I get you one?"

She nodded and smiled.

I liked working with her. I loved the feeling of being valued by the people I helped. I wanted to understand what she was talking about, but it was difficult. I got two glasses of red wine and went back.

"I'm not going to ask you about the course again," she said, referring to her coach training program, which she had been trying to get me to sign up for.

"Nobody here asked me if I was certified," I said.

"Of course not. They like being your students. But that's not your future. You've got much more potential than that."

"I've been a founder, chairman and CEO," I said. "Becoming a coach feels..."

"Small? Less... valuable?"

"Well, I wouldn't put it in those words." But yes, that was it.

She looked out at the city lights and leaned against the railing.

"You're going to have to decide what you want," she said. "I'll give you as much work as I can. But at some point, you won't be able to go further, without fully committing."

"I am committed. I love this work."

"If you want to transform people's lives... you need to be in constant transformation yourself." She paused. "Right now, though... you're very committed to be in your status quo. When that shifts, a whole new world will open for you. I can see it already. You have good instincts with people. Your intuition is great. And you see the best in others." She stopped and stared at me. "I won't say anything more. You do what you want."

That sounded too permanent. I didn't want her to be upset.

"I'll look at the coaching program again," I said.

She sighed. I guess I wasn't very persuasive.

A burst of laughter and loud voices caught my attention. Several startup founders standing at a bar table near us were doing shots and slamming their glasses on the table.

"You must have been around their age when you started your company," Misha said.

They were in their early to mid-thirties. I nodded at Misha.

"What did you love about being a CEO?" She asked.

"I guess... to start... I got to create my own job, using all of my skills and qualities. There weren't many jobs in the Southern French countryside for international software executives, so I created my dream job."

"And... you've said before... you didn't want to work in your wife's vineyard."

"It was her parents."

"Beautiful place."

"One of the most beautiful places I know."

"You can always move back to France."

"That was my dream as a younger man. It's over."

"You can do whatever you want."

"I don't want to go back. That dream is over."

She nodded and looked away.

Living in France, on a vineyard, and building a global company — all of that was a younger man's dream. When I first moved to France, when Val was a baby, I thought I would be there the rest of my life. I had no idea the dream would someday end, and another chapter of life would have to be written in a very different place. Circumstances took me very far from anywhere I had lived before, to this big, modern city still holding onto a bit of its rainforest jungle.

"So, from wanting to create a job for yourself," Misha said, "you ended up creating lots of jobs."

"Oh man! That was SO amazing! I loved being able to create a tech company out in a rural area that gave so many people jobs. I loved being involved in every major decision of my company — hiring, designing the technology, filing patents, driving marketing and sales, fundraising, dealing with shareholders, strategizing an exit. It was amazingly heady."

"They probably have all of those feelings as well," Misha nodded toward the young entrepreneurs doing shots.

"I'm sure they do."

"It's going to be very hard to give all that up. I see why you're struggling."

The men doing shots reminded me of some of the people I

had hired.

"I think... what I loved most as CEO... was the thing I also see in coaching. Watching people grow. I tried to hire people less for their past experience, and more for their desire to grow."

She looked out at the city skyline. After a long moment, she looked back at me.

"I forgot to mention, I met up with your old CTO a couple weeks ago."

"Which one?"

"Your first."

"Thomas?"

She nodded.

"I haven't spoken to him in ages."

Thomas had hired our first programmers and built the first generation of our product. He was also one of the first people I fired, when we needed a more experienced CTO. Looking back, the decision was extremely ordinary in the fast-paced life of a start-up. But even after — what is it, fifteen years at least — I still felt I had failed him. It had been my responsibility to help him grow into his role, and I had failed.

"He said you were his most memorable boss."

I snorted.

"He said you fired him."

I nodded. That must have been an interesting conversation, complaining to Misha about his ex-boss.

"He said... being fired was the best thing that could have happened."

"What? The best thing?"

"I'm sure it was painful... for both of you. He said he now knows he had been too inexperienced for the role. And he had been struggling to hide that from you and everyone else. Firing me freed me... that's what he said. He was able to rebuild after that."

"Wow."

I was surprised to feel relieved. Had I held onto guilt all this time? My mind was a jumble of thoughts.

"He's running a big team now, covering a large region. All of Europe, Middle East, and Africa."

"That's great." The guilt had somehow turned to pride.

"He told me something you told him, and that he has remembered throughout his career. A quote. Let's see if I can remember... Perfection is achieved, not when there is nothing more to add..."

"... but when there is nothing left to take away," I finished the rest of the quote.

She laughed and nodded.

"Saint-Exupery," I was surprised he still remembered that quote by the author of The Little Prince.

"Apparently, it has been with him all these years," she said.

I felt myself sinking into a deep sense of satisfaction and peacefulness.

"You know, people need to feel seen. You saw your people as they could be. And you demanded they be their best. That's powerful. And that's exactly how you've been mentoring these startup founders. You see things in them that they don't even see. That's very inspiring. That's why I know you will be a great coach."

I hadn't thought of it like that. But I loved what she was saying.

"You created a company in the vineyards..."

"It wasn't really IN the vineyards."

"... when your daughter was a baby, and now Val is twenty-five, all grown up and living her own life."

An adult yes, but only since a few short years.

"Misha, I'm so worried. Why did she have to get involved in relief efforts? There are professionals for that."

"No news is good news, right?"

"It's been weeks."

"I'd be terrified."

"I keep wondering if she has enough drinking water. Every morning when I wake up, I check for a message. And then I search for pictures of relief workers in Samoa."

"I've looked too. But I stopped. It's just tsunami disaster porn."

The view was so beautiful up here. It was amazing these tall buildings were built on reclaimed land that was in the sea only a few years ago. What a stark contrast to what Val must have been experiencing in Samoa.

A handheld bell rang somewhere in the crowd, its shrill sound breaking through the hum of people drinking and talking, like a Salvation Army volunteer standing next to a donation box on a busy sidewalk. I turned and saw a hotel employee ringing an old-fashioned bell and holding up a sign with my name.

"Over here," I waved at the man.

"Aidan Perez?"

"That's me."

"A message for you." He handed me an envelope.

Inside was an invitation to a conference called "Resilience and Reinvention: Thriving In The Twenty-First Century." There was a handwritten message on the card: Congratulations on the startup conference. We'd love to have you speak at ours. Please call me. Agnes Lim

"Everything OK?" Misha asked.

I nodded and put the invitation back into the envelope.

"So? What is it?"

"Have you heard of a conference called Resilience and Reinvention?"

"Of course. That's a big one."

"They've been trying to contact me. They want me to give a talk."

"Really?"

"You look surprised."

"It's just that... they have a very stringent selection process."

"I've spoken at lots of conferences."

"Banking conferences."

"And?"

"That's your old life. This would be... very different."

"Now I can step into my new life; and talk about reinvention."

She didn't look convinced. For good reason. I haven't reinvented myself. I'm just... languishing... as she said.

"You always have an interesting perspective," Misha said, "always new and different."

She was trying to be nice.

"Find out who is on the selection committee. If you can meet a committee member before the selection, maybe..."

"Yeah." I cut her off, not wanting to hear the rest.

I knew I was stuck. I hadn't really committed to reinventing myself. Misha knew me well. Other people didn't. They didn't see the mess underneath my confident outer persona. I looked at the card again. The conference was in three months. There was little chance I would have much to say in such a short time.

I finished my glass and picked up my bag.

"It's getting late for you," Misha said.

I smiled.

"Imagine being out after dark," she said as I walked away. "Lots of people do it."

I left as the rooftop bar was becoming busier. Misha would be busy networking until the bar closed.

That's when the second part of my dream snapped into my memory. It happened while waiting at a crosswalk, surrounded by a crowd of executives waiting to cross the road. In that exact moment, the rest of my dream snapped into my mind, as a fully formed memory.

In my dream, I was on a busy street in a big city, standing at a crosswalk, just like here. Executives in suits and ties waited for me to help them cross the road. That was my job — helping people cross the road safely, from one side to the other. Bizarrely, I was dressed in a white robe, like a monk, giving my work an almost spiritual quality. But my shoes were dusty, as if I had walked a long way to get to this crosswalk.

While the first dream with the eagle felt predictive, this second part felt prescriptive. As if my subconscious was warning me that my current path led to decay and death, and that the way out would be to serve others by helping them cross from one side of the road to the other — whatever that meant. It felt like this was related to the mentoring and coaching work I was doing.

The dreamscape hanging in the background was so present it felt increasingly real and true; solid, in a way. It didn't quite make complete sense yet, but I was sure it was about to become clear.

That would happen several days after the rooftop conversation, during a lunch meeting with a group of Misha's friends who called themselves the Nomads.

Accepting the Call

It was my turn, as the newest member of the Nomads, to select the venue for our monthly meeting. I chose my favourite restaurant in Little India, which always reminded me of Val, because she used to want to go there all the time. It was a small place with a private dining room in the back, where we sat.

The Nomads were a group of four senior executives from various non-competing industries who met regularly to share challenges and breakthroughs.

The waiter who always served me, Amit, poked his head in the door and looked at me quizzically.

"Not yet," I said, "we're waiting for two more people."

He nodded and disappeared.

Three of us were already there — myself, my friend Misha sitting across from me, and a lady name Joanna. David and Rajiv arrived moments later, completing the group. Misha had introduced me to the group. Other than her, I didn't know any of the others.

David introduced himself with a French accent.

"Français?" I asked.

"Toi aussi?" He nodded.

"Almost," I responded in French. "So far, France is the country I lived in the longest."

David switched back to English. "Since you've already started, and you're new, why don't you go first today?"

"Uh... sure. What do I do?"

"Each person shares something challenging that happened since we last met," David said.

"Or a breakthrough you're proud of," Joanna added. "Anything you're excited about."

"We have a rule," Misha said. "When someone is sharing, the others refrain from giving advice, comments, suggestions, and even talking. So, the person sharing can speak without interruption."

I nodded.

"How about you start with an introduction," David said.

"OK. My name is Aidan Perez. Born in the US, but I've lived most of my life overseas. I lived in France for twenty years, where I created a tech company. I sold my company a few years ago and moved to Singapore. I chose Singapore because I had lots of business contacts and friends in Singapore. Plus, my daughter was going to the university here at that time, so it was a great place to build a new life."

I talked about the project I had just finished, mentoring startup founders with Misha, and how that made me feel useful.

"The struggles building my company suddenly seem worthwhile," I said. "The mistakes I made feel valuable when I share what I learned with others. And especially when I see others benefit from my experience. That's so fulfilling."

I glanced around the table, waiting for someone to say something.

"Thank you," I said.

They were still silent. What were they waiting for?

"That's it for me..."

"I was hoping to hear something... challenging," David said.

Joanna and Rajiv nodded. Misha avoided eye contact.

"There must be something you're struggling with," David said.

Was I supposed to dump out everything bothering me?

"OK... where to start? I haven't decided really what I want to do next." I glanced at Misha. "Mentoring startup founders was easy. It felt like a hobby, using skills I developed running my own company. I think I want to do something more challenging. But I'm not sure I want to actually become a certified coach. Who needs yet another coach, right?"

Misha was looking down at the table again.

"But... actually... what's really on my mind... is my daughter. Do you all talk about personal things too?"

Joanna smiled at me and nodded.

"Valérie — Val — is twenty-five. She's in Samoa, where she teaches high school English and French. But I haven't heard from her in a few weeks. She's in a remote area, helping people recover from last year's tsunami. I knew there wasn't much internet connection right now. But I didn't realise how long periods without hearing her voice would make me feel."

There was silence around the table, making me feel I might have shared too much. David glanced at me, as if he expected more.

"Val and I became very close over the last few years. We shared an apartment when she was going to the university. We became even closer than when we lived in France. Of course, I was traveling all the time for work back then. Anyway, she originally planned on moving back to France after graduation — she's half French — but instead she left on an around-the-world trip that eventually took her to where she is today, Samoa."

That was much more than I had intended to share. I looked at the door, wondering when the waiter would be back.

"That's pretty much it," I said.

"You must miss her," David said.

"Desperately. My chest aches. I never knew I could miss someone so much."

"How do you know each other?" Joanna pointed at Misha and me.

"Wow, that goes back a while. Six years?"

"More like eight," Misha said, "maybe nine."

"I was still in France. I had a software development team in

Singapore, and regional sales and marketing. I wanted to do a team building workshop in Singapore. Someone introduced me to Misha. And we became friends after that."

"Now you're trying to do the same thing as me," Misha said. "I must have done a good job."

I laughed.

"Later, we brought Misha to France to work with our team there. She's still in touch with some of my old colleagues."

Everyone looked satisfied now.

"So? Am I in?"

Joanna laughed, and David gave me a thumbs up.

"Thank you for the audition," I pretended to bow from my seat.

David went next. He talked about how hard it was to get several people who worked for him to take on more responsibility. He was a French-North African Israeli who headed Human Resources at a technology company, after spending years doing similar work at Google and eBay.

"I want to empower them," he said, "but they always want me to tell them what to do. I don't want to do that. I want them to find solutions on their own. Either I don't have the right people, or something I'm doing isn't working."

He glanced at me and paused. Was he expecting me to say something? Then he turned to Misha.

"I'd love to hear one of your coaching questions," he said. "Would you be up to that?"

"How about Aidan? He's got great intuition and coaching instincts."

David looked at me, his eyebrows raised, waiting for my response.

"I don't think that would be appropriate," I said.

Misha looked at me, amused.

"I like that Aidan likes this restaurant," she said.

"I mainly come here because my daughter loves this place. When she was still in Singapore, we ate here together a couple times a week."

"There is more to it than that." Misha glanced around at the pictures on the walls, and the objects scattered artfully around the room. "Do you know that the restaurant is inspired by a very old Mumbai service that delivers lunches to workers?" Misha pointed at the traditional tiered lunch boxes placed decoratively on shelves.

"The Dabbawallas of Mumbai," Rajiv said. "Did you notice how all the waiters wear white caps? It's the Dabbawalla cap."

"To me it looks like something Ghandi wore," I said.

The cap is pointed in front and back, and can be folded flat when not worn, like military caps, but white. I noticed that Amit wore his cap tilted forward, covering almost all of his forehead, while the other waiters wore theirs a bit tilted back and to the side.

"The restaurant probably offers free meals," Rajiv said, "like a soup kitchen."

Misha nodded. "We're subsidising their meals."

When I first came here, I had noticed workers eating here and wondered how they could afford a meal — the restaurant wasn't cheap.

"I saw a sign for kitchen volunteers a few weeks ago," I said.

"Service and contribution," Misha said.

"Dabbawallas are intensely focused on perfect service," Rajiv said. "They deliver food from a worker's home to the worker, wherever they are in Mumbai, with almost zero error. They see their work as an almost spiritual practice."

"Aidan is dedicated to serving others too," Misha said. "Hence, we are here today."

Rajiv nodded at me, as if he saw me differently now, in a way that surprised him.

"It's pretty simple," Rajiv said, "serve others... live life fully."

"So?" David turned to me.

"I can try."

David nodded.

"This is about empowering your team, right?"

"That's all I talked about."

I could hear Misha's voice in my head... Don't teach! Ask powerful questions!

"OK... how would you rate yourself as an empowering leader, from one to ten?"

David thought for a moment. "Maybe seven or eight. My team would probably give me a lower number." He laughed.

"Got it. Where would you like to be?"

"A nine would be great."

"And... if I were to ask you... what is the word that comes after the verb delegate? What is it that you delegate?"

He looked confused.

"If you were to complete the sentence, I delegate... blank... what word would fit in there, for you? Hold on... let me see if I still have this..." I searched my phone's notes for a paragraph I had often used with my own managers. "Ah... here it is. What word would fill in the blank?" I read out the note. "When you delegate -blank- you free up your time and achieve more daily. Delegating -blank- is one of the most important and effective management skills. The inability to delegate -blank- is one of the biggest problems managers face at all levels. Without the skill, it is impossible for you to advance to higher positions of responsibility. Delegating -blank- maximises your own productivity and value, as well as the productivity of your staff. You create an atmosphere of confidence and trust. Subordinates will come to think of you as an effective leader who respects their contribution."

"Tasks," David said. "I delegate tasks."

I waited a moment for that to sink in.

"Oh," he smiled. "I get it. That's not very empowering."

I nodded.

"So... what...what SHOULD I be delegating? If not tasks?"

"What would your word be, instead of tasks... for something more empowering?"

"Results," Rajiv jumped in.

"I get it," David said.

"Authority," Rajiv added. "That's the dictionary definition of empowerment. Delegating power or authority."

David took out his phone and began typing something. Then he put it down. He had a look of satisfaction, like he knew where to go next.

"You can ask your team to rate you on a scale of one to ten," I said, wondering if Misha would consider that teaching. "Where one corresponds to delegating tasks and ten is delegating results, outcomes, authority. Ask them where they generally see you on that scale. And discuss where on the scale would be most effective. I call it the management to leadership scale."

I heard Misha's voice booming in my head — You're teaching again! Stop teaching!

He started typing in his phone again.

"Does that help?"

David nodded, still typing.

"I learned this years ago," I said, "it feels great when people need you to tell them what tasks to do and how to get them done. You're needed for your knowledge and experience. But that keeps them stuck in lower levels of delegation. When you delegate authority, they need you to be clear and unwavering about the results you want. You're still needed, but not for the same thing. And that creates empowerment."

"Thank you," David said without looking up. "Who's next?"

After a brief pause, Joanna spoke up.

I learned that Joanna was a marketing executive at a company I knew well, which happened to have been my client a few years earlier. As far as I knew, her company was still using software I had sold them.

Joanna talked about her ongoing challenges with her new role managing five different functions, where for the last fifteen years she was responsible for only one of those functions. She now felt unqualified and couldn't understand how people could look up to her as a leader when she didn't understand their day-to-day activities.

"How do I manage people doing jobs I don't understand? What if they discover I'm not an expert in their area? How do I know if they're doing their jobs right? How do I know if they're even working? Sometimes it feels like I have to herd a bunch of teenagers."

Joanna paused and looked up at the door.

"When is the waiter coming?" Joanna's voice instantly shifted, regaining the certainty of someone in charge.

I went to the door and looked out into the main room, trying to get the waiter's attention. Amit glanced at me from the far end of the room, as he set food down on another table. I waved, he nodded back.

When I sat back down, Joanna continued. She explained how she constantly searched for evidence that people didn't trust her. Small remarks were seen as judgment of her weaknesses. The more she felt her team didn't trust her, the less she trusted them. Where she used to be decisive, she now found herself hesitating, doubting her judgment. Previously confident and outspoken, she suddenly became silent in meetings. It sounded like she was on the verge of giving up. I felt like telling her that somebody must have thought she was capable enough to take on more. There must surely have been people who believed in her. Who were they?

"I have to be good at my job without being an expert across all these new departments. How in the world do I do that? It's like... I have to be an orchestra conductor. But the musicians are a bunch of teenage kids." She laughed.

Joanna talked about another person from her team quitting, someone she had hoped would take on a larger role. She told us that her team had the lowest engagement scores across the company.

She sighed and paused. After a moment, the silence started to feel uncomfortable. Where in the world was Amit? This was the perfect time for him to pop in and take our order.

"I guess they still think I'm cold, and a bit too direct," she said. "But managers have to be tough and direct. We shouldn't have to deal with emotions at work. That's... that's what I've always been taught."

The waiter finally came into the room.

"Sorry to keep you waiting," he said. "You're waiting for the waiter." He paused, looking at me as if I was supposed to understand. "You're waiting for the waiter. So... does that make you the waiter?"

"Dad joke," I smiled to the others, feeling the need to apologize for my choice of venue.

David laughed.

Amit had said something cheesy the first time I came here. I immediately liked him and this restaurant. Amit appeared to be in his fifties. I imagine he had been practicing his jokes for years.

"I always order the Thali," I said, referring to the set meal served in a collection of small bowls on a platter.

"I'll have the same," Rajiv said to the waiter.

"Make that three," David said. He closed his menu without looking at it and handed it back to Amit.

"That's too much food for me," Misha said.

She and Joanna chose a dish to share. Amit the waiter stared at the two women, waiting for more.

"That's all," Joanna said.

"You're eating light," the waiter said. "Can I bring you one Philips LED?"

He tried to keep a deadpan face, but his barely concealed smile showed he was quite pleased with that one.

Joanna looked at me and actually giggled. I felt a little embarrassed for Amit.

"I actually like his jokes," I said after Amit stepped out.

"You're a dad joke kind of guy," Misha laughed, then turned to the others. "My son laughs at the jokes, so Aidan tells even more. It's so cringey."

As we waited for the food, I turned to Joanna. "By the way, is Vincent Goh still at your company?"

"You mean... the Vincent Goh on our executive committee?"

"I knew him when he was my client years ago."

"He's a big chief now. I don't know him personally."

After everyone's food arrived, Misha wanted to go next.

"Wait," Joanna said. "Can I get a little bit of coaching first? From Aidan?"

Misha nodded.

"Me again?" I glanced at Misha, wondering if I was stepping on her toes. Clearly, she was the one who normally asked coaching questions here.

"Joanna wants to hear you," Misha said.

"OK," I turned to Joanna. "You said something very intriguing earlier."

Her eyebrows were raised in curiosity and her eyes sparkled.

"You said you needed to be an orchestra conductor."

"Yes," she said, "but I can't."

"Do you play an instrument?"

"I used to play the piano, a long time ago," she laughed. "I wanted to be a concert pianist. That was way back when I was a teenager."

"So, what is it about being a conductor that feels impossible?"

"They have to be experts in every instrument. I'm not. I don't know what most of my departments actually do in their day-to-day work."

"And to be completely clear," I said, "does that mean you believe that a conductor should know how to play every instrument in the orchestra?"

She looked at me like it was a trick question. I resisted breaking the silence so as not to interrupt her thought process, and to let her think about it fully.

"Yes, definitely," she said.

Misha and David both smiled. Even Rajiv looked amused. When she saw their reactions, Joanna looked even more confused.

"What if that's not true?" I said. Misha's voice popped up in my head again, *Don't teach.*

"It's not," Rajiv jumped in.

Joanna looked at David, he shook his head too.

"Conductors don't know how to play all the instruments," Rajiv said. "Some of them are really bad musicians."

"Maybe your role isn't to master each person's expertise," I said, trying not to sound like a professor. "Maybe your role is to understand your organization's vision and goals so clearly that you can communicate the music to your various teams. You only need to trust that they can play their various instruments masterfully."

"Spot on," David said.

"Conductors know how to play all instruments," said Joanna. "I'm sure of it."

"I have an idea," David said, "do you know any professional musicians?"

"A couple friends from university."

"Why don't you ask them?"

Joanna nodded. She typed something into her phone. Maybe she was already texting a friend.

Misha went next.

"No need for an intro," she said, "everyone knows me."

"I love hearing your story," Joanna said.

Rajiv and David both agreed.

"The short version then," Misha laughed. "I was born in Edinburgh, where my mother is from. My father was Indian, from Mumbai. I grew up mainly in Hong Kong, where we lived throughout my childhood. I'm a coach and trainer. And I run a training program for new coaches... a program which I still hope Aidan will join."

I laughed.

Misha looked just as Indian as Rajiv and Amit but spoke with an international expat accent that could shift and change depending on who she was speaking with.

"The most challenging thing right now isn't my work," Misha said. "It's... my son."

How much was she going to share about Matt in this semi-professional environment?

"He's sixteen," she paused, looking around at the others. When she looked at me, I nodded. "He... Matt... was diagnosed with depression. He's on medication."

I knew that Misha blamed herself, even though she denied it.

The others listened silently. Joanna looked at Misha with a wrinkled forehead. Rajiv mainly stared at the backs of his hands.

"The other day... he told me", she blew air out, as if expelling something bad, "that he wants to see his father."

When did that happen? I hadn't heard this before.

"He doesn't even remember him. Why would he want to see him?"

As far as I knew, Matt's father was in the UK someplace, but I couldn't remember where.

"I told him he can see whoever he wants when he's eighteen. Besides, I don't even know how to contact him. Matt blew up and had one of his meltdowns." She paused, her face hard and tough. "I'm just baggage, he said. I've had enough of you, he said.

And then... the worst part. He kept shouting, Misha, this is what I want! Listen to what I want, Misha!"

"It was a meltdown," I blurted out, forgetting I was supposed to stay quiet. "You know he didn't mean it."

"Those were exactly the words his father used to shout at me. How does a three-year-old boy absorb that kind of behaviour and then vomit it out more than a decade later?" She paused and drank a sip of water. "Why are teenage boys so obsessed with father figures? He doesn't need the man."

This was a window into her past that I had never seen so clearly. I always knew her marriage had been difficult, but she had never wanted to share details. I felt dizzy and nauseous. I couldn't imagine how difficult things must have been for Matt. I knew he needed a father figure. That was very evident in our interactions. I didn't know he needed more than that.

"I'm not going to ask for coaching or feedback," Misha said to me. "I don't want some question, like how I think Matt might rate me as a mother from one to ten."

I nodded, relieved. That was pretty much the one coaching type of question I was most comfortable with. Anyway, I couldn't see the purpose of sharing such personal and vulnerable details in a professional environment.

It was Rajiv's turn next. Rajiv was an Indian business CEO who lived between his textile factory in Mumbai, and his home in Singapore, where he also ran his family's investment business.

"I can't get that young man out of my mind," he said.

That would be a twenty-two-year-old worker who was electrocuted while trying to repair one of the machines. Misha had told me about the accident a few days earlier. The young man's death was the factory's latest fatality.

"TV crews are camped outside the factory gates," Rajiv said, "blocking the street. They're waiting for the next accident." He shook his head and sighed. "Our health and safety standards have been audited. Several times. All of our procedures have been analysed. Improvements were made over the past year. I have paid millions of dollars to management consultants. And we implemented all of their recommendations. We've done everything." He threw his hands up in an I give up gesture. "Even with all that... people are still dying. What else am I supposed to do?" He pushed his Thali platter away, which he had hardly touched. "He was only twenty-two."

The skin at the back of my neck was clammy and my face was cold and sweaty. My throat felt constricted and scratchy. I recognized what was happening — I was having an empathic response triggered by my brain's mirror neurons. My body was attempting to mirror the emotions it intuitively felt Rajiv was experiencing. I recognized shame.

After Rajiv finished sharing, there was a period of silence. Then he turned toward me.

"What do your instincts tell you about my situation?"

My work had never exposed me to issues like the ones facing Rajiv. I didn't understand a thing about people working in his factory and the industrial machinery they had to operate.

"I don't know anything about workplace safety," I said. "The stakes are too high. I am so far out of my depth." But then a flash of intuition came. "I could ask you one question."

He nodded.

"How would you rate your commitment to safety?"

Rajiv put a finger to his lips, as if he was thinking.

"Very high," he said.

"A number?"

He pressed his lips together and slowly shook his head.

"Very high... nine."

"That's high," I said. "If it was lower, the accidents would be higher, I'm sure."

I could stop now. But Rajiv looked at me, as if waiting for more.

"How about your team? How committed would you say they are?"

"Surveys show the whole organization is highly committed to safety. I'd say eight out of ten, across the board."

"What if that's why people are dying? What if... that one digit... nine instead of ten... represents something missing in your commitment?"

Rajiv stared at me.

"What if your team is missing something too? Not much, eight is already high. But it's not ten. What if that's why people are dying?"

Rajiv's face turned red.

"I can't be ten out of ten committed," he blurted. "That's impossible! You don't understand... workers do crazy things! Most of them aren't educated! I can't be on their backs every moment."

I nodded.

"They do crazy things! If somebody needs to get to the other end of the factory, they'll jump on a forklift going by. They know they're not supposed to, but they do it anyway. They should be able to take care of themselves. They're adults! Not children! I can't be standing behind every single person... to make sure they don't do stupid things!"

"I... I agree."

"So, what the hell are you talking about?"

"You're right," I said. "I'm sorry."

"Ten out of ten," he muttered, shaking his head, holding his arms crossed.

I noticed David fidgeting in his chair and looking at his watch. I should have stopped a couple minutes earlier. Now we were ending my first Nomad group meeting on a sour note.

David left for a meeting, followed closely by Misha and Joanna. Rajiv lingered a bit. It felt like he had more to say to me. I just wanted to leave.

"And yourself," he said, his voice calmer now, "how committed are you to being a coach?"

"I... I'm..."

"Yeah, I thought so. You're a successful startup founder playing around with being a coach." He stood up to leave, then turned to face me. "Soon, you're going to join a few boards. That's what people like you do. You become a board member. Maybe you'll start another company. This coaching thing is temporary. You're not committed."

Then he left.

He was right. I wasn't fully committed. I wasn't as serious as

I could be about my coaching work, and certainly wasn't acting as a diligent professional, learning new tools and striving toward mastery.

The restaurant was almost empty now. The cashier at the front door briefly glanced at me above her glasses as she counted the money in her till.

"I wanted to thank our waiter, but I don't see him."

"He's gone," she said.

"Ah?"

"He has another job. He helps us out at lunch."

Now that was commitment and hard work.

"How much?"

"Your friend paid already," she said.

"Already?"

"The European man."

That would be David.

I noticed a small stack of pamphlets next to the cash register, printed on yellow paper. It was the title in big block letters that caught my eye: "*FIVE STEPS TO JOYFUL WISDOM*. Based on the three universal characteristics of existence: impermanence, suffering, and no-self."

There was something familiar about the big title, the way joyful and wisdom were used together. I had seen other Buddhist and Hindu pamphlets in restaurants and coffee shops, but they didn't stand out to me the way this one did.

"Take one," the cashier said.

I picked up a pamphlet and turned it over, looking for a price.

"It's free."

On my way home in a cab, I opened the pamphlet. It felt more like a manuscript photocopied and stapled together like an academic paper. Thirty-six pages organised in five-chapter headings that sounded ancient and modern at the same time: One — Entering The Path; Two — Seeing Into The Beautiful Abyss Of The Mind; Three — Detaching From The Illusion Of Self; Four — Relinquishing The Lust For Control; Five — Embracing The Joy Of A Lifelong Beginner.

The first chapter, Entering The Path, started with a myth I

knew well, but with a twist. Melanesians of the South Pacific is-
lands have a legend about the time when humans were immortal,
shedding their skin and becoming young again, over, and over. I
knew this myth because it was one of my wife's favorites. I had
heard the same story many times, but never as sensually detailed
as in this book. The legend, which the manuscript called The Immortal Ones, was told from the perspective of an old woman whose
daughter died soon after giving birth, leaving the woman to care
for her granddaughter. Chantal would have loved this version since
it mirrored her own life. Chantal's mother had died in childbirth,
and she was raised by her grandparents.

As I read the book — the stories, advice, and exercises —
I felt like I was re-discovering something that had always been
within me, but had been lost, or, rather, forgotten. When the taxi
stopped, what seemed only like moments later, I was surprised to
see I was already home.

Entering the Path

*An external shock challenges a person's worldview, forcing an
internal change which he or she resists. People at the beginning of the
Journey To Joyful Wisdom become aware they are stuck in their comfort zone, avoiding change. They begin to see how they expect others to
change, not themselves. Often, they are respected publicly, but feel like
impostors. When the pressure for change is strong, introspection begins, leading to awareness that the person knows less than previously
thought. While in this stage, they commonly encounter emotions of de-
nial, anxiety, anger, and shame. If the goal is important enough, they
will push through to the next stage of their Journey To Joyful Wisdom.*

The chapter resonated with me from beginning to end. It was
as if it was written to describe the change I was experiencing.

The manuscript described how every transformation journey
begins with a call to change, an invitation to begin the adventure.
Maybe we realise we're making the same mistake over and over.

Maybe it's a string of failed relationships with people who we suddenly see are curiously alike. Or maybe we get passed over for a promotion... again. There is a growing sense of needing to do something different. I wasn't familiar with the Hindu and Buddhist mythological examples in the manuscript, but I got the idea. It was like Harry Potter receiving an acceptance letter from Hogwarts, or Luke Skywalker finding Princess Leia's holographic message inside the robot R2D2.

I realised I hadn't heard the call to change until it was repeated multiple times, in various ways that grew in intensity. First there were the dreams, then the conversation about Thomas, then Misha and the startups, and then just today, with the Nomads and Rajiv's words, challenging me to take coaching seriously.

The manuscript explained how people often refuse the call to change, for lots of reasons. You get to stay in your comfort zone. There's no risk of trying something new which could fail. You also get to keep your image, because you're playing a role that you're familiar with. Any attempt at a new role or a new way of interacting with others could result in failure. In some cases, you even get sympathy for staying in the status quo ("I can't believe they gave the job to someone else! Again! You definitely should have gotten it.") In general, you don't have to take responsibility for the situation. You might be able to blame others, or your organization, or even blame yourself for your own lack of abilities. You get to be right about how you see the world ("Employees don't want to be empowered, they just want me to tell them what to do; they like being micromanaged, it makes them feel safe.") and right about your capabilities ("If I don't micromanage everything, I will lose control; what then would I be good for?") All of these beliefs mix together in various doses, creating a mindset sludge that's hard to escape.

When the need to change becomes unbearable, people usually find the courage to let go of an old identity and adopt a new one. There is nothing in this world more beautiful than watching someone blossom into a new phase of their life, especially after they held onto their old selves and resisted change for a long time.

The manuscript also had exercises. The first one was titled Who Will You Be At A Hundred?

Who Will You Be At A Hundred?

This exercise helps you let go of the illusion of permanence. Who you are today is not who you were twenty, thirty or forty years ago, or who your joyful self will be in the future. During your lifetime, you can follow your heart and switch careers and industries multiple times, learn new skills along the way, and forget details that used to be important and useful earlier in life. As you grow older, you will develop the art of dumping baggage, old jobs, and expired relationships, because you can't carry all that stuff decades into the future. The intellectual mind can't extrapolate beyond a few years — looking far into the future forces your brain to tap into dream visions, intuition, and your heart's joy-filled desire for connection.

When I started this exercise, I immediately thought of my grandmother, who had lived to ninety-seven. She had been active all her life, even to the last few years. She loved visiting us when I was growing up, in Cairo, Rome, and Paris. Whenever she did, she would invariably tack on other side trips to nearby countries, like Jordan and Greece, or even further away, like Russia and China.

If I was lucky enough to have her long age genes, I could expect to live several more decades. Was fifty now the mid-point of my life? I might have the equivalent of another entire career ahead of me, spanning several more decades, maybe even longer than the career I had so far.

Looking forward to who you might be at a hundred will reveal a roadmap of possible paths from where you are today. It will loosen the grip of the need to find your ideal life purpose at this moment. What if we have many life purposes? What if there is no one single lifelong purpose? Free from the search for an overarching purpose, you can find the joy in whatever you are doing now.

Where will I live over the next decades? I had already lived two-thirds of my life outside the United States. My life seems to have been a progressive journey east, bringing me to my latest home in Singapore. Further east would be China, Japan, Korea, the Philippines, Australia, and New Zealand. Would I choose instead to go back to a place I had lived before? Nowhere felt like home. Without roots, I could drift anywhere.

I read through the instructions then settled in for a mindfulness session. Eyes closed, breathing in through my nostrils, feeling the coolness at the back of my throat, and noticing the natural pauses in between breaths.

Breath in... pause... then breath out.

Noticing the rhythm.

The beautiful silence during the pause. Was there a touch of joy in the pause? Or was that the influence of the manuscript?

The center of language is silence.

I let a smile come to the edges of my mouth, as the instructions suggested.

Yes, there was definitely a touch of joyfulness in each pause between breaths.

The center of emotion is acceptance.

Was it possible to relax just a little bit more? As soon as I asked this question, I felt my body sink even further into my sofa.

Now — imagine you're a hundred years old.
You're outside walking on a path along a boulevard.
You're on your way to a venue where you will be giving a talk.
The path is lined with tall trees.
Imagine the wind blowing through the bright green leaves.
A red bird sings as you walk by.
Bright coloured vehicles drive by silently — blue, yellow, red.

Your senses are filled with joyful aliveness.

When you arrive at the venue, people immediately usher you to the stage.

The MC introduces you and you step onto the big red dot on the carpet.

You look out at the audience.

There are so many people here; they want to hear you speak; they want to hear your story.

Whatever you have been working on has become a success.

You have struggled for so long to get here.

You stuck through difficult times; persevered through doubts and fears and challenges.

And now you're here.

Feel the relief.

Take a moment to feel proud.

You begin speaking.

What are you speaking about? What are you sharing?

What have you been passionate about all these years?

When you finish, the room stands and applauds.

Enjoy the joyful aliveness of this moment.

I could visualise the whole scene, like watching a movie. But I didn't know what I was talking about. I found myself daydreaming about the bright coloured trees, birds, and cars. And the TED Talk styled red dot on the carpet. The process was relaxing, mainly due to the breath meditation, but it didn't reveal any breakthrough insights.

The manuscript was short. I finished reading it in a couple hours. It felt like I had just been offered the tourist's version of a Thali platter, with a few very small bowls instead of the normal meal. Where could I find more? The manuscript didn't have a name, address, or phone number. What kind of temple would put out a brochure that wasn't designed to attract new people?

Later that evening, after dinner, I went for a walk to enjoy the slightly cooler evening temperatures, which of course never really go down much in the tropics. I thought again of my grand-mother. She was a toddler during the First World War, a young adult during the Second, and just a little older than me when Armstrong walked on the moon. She had lived through the Great Depression, homesteaded in Texas and New Mexico, flown on jets all over the world, ridden a camel in Jordan, walked along the Great Wall of China, visited Moscow before the Berlin Wall came down, and spent several summers at my home in France. What dramatic transformations she lived through. Always joyful and optimistic. Profoundly alive. Every moment of her life. At least that's how it seemed to me.

The nighttime frog songs had started, croaking from drainage ditches and private Koi ponds. I reflected on the changes I might experience throughout my own life. That's when the vision came to me.

I saw myself at sunrise, on a wooden balcony, looking out over a forest toward the sea in the distance, holding a cup of coffee. I was at an offsite retreat where I was about to start doing my work, which had something to do with coaching individuals and groups. It felt like somewhere on the East Coast of Australia.

A handful of people were at the retreat and would soon be waking up. I was about to facilitate a workshop for yet another batch of what seemed like religious leaders. But they weren't church leaders, or even religious in the sense we understand today. They were senior executives of future versions of today's multinationals, new types of organisations focused on the well-being of all stakeholders and the planet, and whose employees were drawn together by a fervent devotion to the organization's cause. Like the faithful of any of today's religions.

My role was to help these people "cross the road," from their old styles of leadership to whatever they wanted to become next. I was hooked. This was my future.

My phone vibrated in my pocket. An unknown caller.

"Hello Mister Perez. This is Agnes Lim. I hope it's not too late."

"Who?"

"Agnes Lim. From the Resilience and Reinvention conference."

"Ah... yes."

"Can you speak?"

"Not really. It's getting late."

"Of course. Can I call you tomorrow?"

I did want to hear what she had to say. A particularly loud frog began croaking wildly.

"Are you out? Maybe tomorrow would be better."

"I'm almost home. Let's talk."

"Great. I won't be long. We really would like you to speak at our conference. Your background is fascinating... Ah... hello?"

"Yes, I'm here. I was on mute. There are lots of frogs out tonight."

She laughed.

"Our attendees want to hear how executives who are... like you... are reinventing themselves."

She meant older. It was clear in her voice.

"What are you doing now, after selling your company?"

"Well, recently I've been mentoring founders."

"You're not launching a new startup?"

"Nope."

"So... you're reinventing... yourself."

"That's it."

"People usually talk about their next big project. Reinventing their industry, stuff like that."

"Just myself, this time."

"Even better. That will really stand out."

"Ok."

"Hmmm... from CEO to mentor. That title, mentor, sounds like something you do until you find your next real job."

"I'm also coaching executives."

"From CEO to coach. That's better. It sounds like a real profession. There's certification involved, which is better than being a mentor. Anybody can say, hey I'm a mentor."

"Yeah... that's right."

"But it's still not... quite... juicy enough."

"What topics are you interested in this year?"

"We're missing something on wisdom in leadership."

"Wisdom?"

The cover of *Five Steps To Joyful Wisdom* popped into my mind.

"It's one of the topics last year's attendees wanted to hear more about," Agnes Lim said.

"That sounds very interesting."

"Lots of companies are struggling with... ethical issues."

"Ethical?"

"Deforestation, animal cruelty, improper marketing of potentially carcinogenic products... that last one is too specific; you probably know who I'm talking about. They're one of our sponsors."

I did not.

"Too much of today's business culture is about heroes... and rainmakers. Most speakers tell personal stories about being dedicated, ambitious, and resilient. These people are hard-working. They go after their business targets aggressively. But they also cut corners sometimes."

"Heroes want to save the day, fix issues on their own."

"Exactly. Hence the ethical concerns."

"They don't like sharing information. And they often have trouble empowering their teams."

"You understand."

"I've been one. I still am in many ways."

"Good, good."

I was back in my apartment building now, walking up the stairs, while trying not to breathe too heavily.

"The hero culture is becoming dangerous," she said.

"And it's not very resilient."

"Especially with all the uncertainty out there. We need a more sustainable culture."

"Less hero and more..."

"Maturity.... and wisdom."

This was sounding so good. Everything she said resonated with me.

"We have had speakers talk about ethics before," Agnes Lim continued. "But people see ethics as a downer topic, a chore."

"It can be dry."

"We'd like a new angle... on wisdom. Something that gets people excited about their personal development. Wisdom is something they can aspire to develop within themselves, which will lead to a greater ethical mindset, without talking directly of ethics. And in turn that would lead to resilience. It would be a whole process of reinvention."

"So, less hero and more... sage."

"Yes!"

"You're looking to develop the Warrior-Sage archetype."

"That sounds spot on. The Warrior-Sage..."

"From hero to sage... leadership skills for an age of uncertainty."

"Is that the title of your talk?"

I was inventing this on the fly. It was more an improvisation than a carefully planned speech.

"I'm working on it right now." This statement was literally true... I was working on it as we spoke.

"That's what I want. From hero to sage..."

"Leadership skills for an age of uncertainty."

"I love it," she said. "Can you send me something I can share with the selection committee? Sometimes they want to meet speakers before giving their approval... but I don't think they'll need to this time."

After hanging up, I prepared an email summarising my talk. It was based on the main themes of Five Steps, using vocabulary that I felt was better suited to a corporate audience. There would be three parts to the talk: un-labeling — letting go of the labels and masks that limit our fullest potential; unleashing — leading and empowering others by relinquishing control; and unlearning — letting go of our expertise and authority, being a beginner again.

I didn't know what would be in the talk, other than the big themes I listed in my email to Agnes Lim. But I was ignited by the conviction that when I get up on that stage, I will have a compelling story to tell. Concrete projects are a great way to drive reinvention. I decided I would immediately embrace being a beginner, and all of the processes and ideas described in *Five Steps To Joyful*

Wisdom. And I would be a beginner in another, completely related area — I decided then to be a student again and sign up for Misha's coach training program. Come on Aidan, get that certification out of the way!

The Immortal Ones - Part 1

The old woman sat crumpled under a small shelter overlooking her fields, built generations ago by her ancestors. She prayed to the spirits of the land.

"Tell me what you want," she whispered, "anything."

Until a few days ago, they had all been working in the fields — the old woman, her husband, their daughter, and their daughter's daughter. Only days ago, the littlest one was taking turns riding on the backs of the adults planting rice. Then the old woman's daughter became too tired to get out of bed. She complained of headaches. A fever last night, then she lost consciousness. The medicine man was summoned along with several elderly village women. They had sent the old woman out to pray in the fields of her ancestors.

A light breeze created waves in the sea of green. A tall bamboo wind chime tapped out a monotonous note in harmony with the ruffling in the trees. Memories of the woman's daughter as a small child came back, following her through these same fields, yanking young green shoots out of the dirt, hiding in the bushes, then laughing when the woman pretended to search for her everywhere.

The woman rubbed her clenched fist against her chest, the heavy air making it hard to breathe.

Had she prayed wrong throughout her life? Maybe not enough? What had she not done right? Was it her pride and stubbornness? Her lack of humility? Is this why her daughter was dying?

As she prayed, she called on the memories of her mother and grandmother. They had sat at this same spot, years ago, praying through their own pain and loss. She was part of an eternal poem, her entire life a single, complex verse of the poem, rhyming with the countless verses before and after her life.

Mournful cries rose from the house, just below the fields. Her daughter was dead. Long, sorrowful voices drifted through the valley, up the hills and across the fields, covering everything in a cold mist, sending sharp stabs of pain through her heart.

Over the following weeks and months, the old couple's life centered on their baby granddaughter. Her giggles and hugs were a powerful healing medicine. Chores became difficult with just the woman and her husband. A young village woman with her own baby moved in with them to nurse the little girl, then left when the girl stopped wanting to nurse. The old woman craved sleep the way young parents do, but without the stamina. Her husband wasn't doing any better. Their chores left undone, chickens disappeared, either wandering away or taken by a predator. Crops rotted in the fields, unharvested.

One day, the woman's older sister came by, 10 years her senior, but looking much younger.

"You should get rid of your wrinkled old skins and become young and energetic again," she said. "Old age wisdom, wrapped inside a new, youthful skin. Very sexy! Yummy-sexy!"

The sister laughed with a naughty look, causing the woman to blush. Her husband sat at the edge of his chair, leaning forward, listening with a smile.

"Bad things might happen," the old woman said.

"You worry too much," her sister smiled. "But that's just you being you."

The old woman turned to her husband. "Aren't you scared?"

He squeezed her hand, causing her tight fist to relax and open.

The woman's sister told them how to find the magical water-fall that cleanses and loosens old skin. She instructed them on the rituals they must follow.

"Soon you will be young again," she said. "Start over fresh. Lose the old memories your skin has been carrying for so many years and which make you heavy and tired."

She winked at them.

"Do you remember when you last made love? Bring that back into your lives now."

The old woman glanced at her husband. He had a big smile on his face, the same smile he had years earlier when they danced together around the village campfire. She decided then that she would do it.

Part Two
Seeing Into The Beautiful Abyss Of The Mind

Shining Sunlight on Trolls

David signed up for the coach training program too, as soon as I announced on the Nomad's group chat that I was doing it. He said he wanted to use coaching skills to become a better leader. I was surprised at how easy it was for him to sign up, when I had resisted it for so long. That's how we ended up together in a downtown hotel conference center along with around thirty other participants.

Listening to each person's introductions at the start of the program, my rough guess was that around half of the people there were like David, looking to develop their coaching skills to become better leaders, and half wanted to become professional coaches. I made some kind of a muddled-up statement about wanting to continue being a tech entrepreneur while coaching on the side. After listening to everyone else's clear intentions, mine sounded like a confused mess.

During one of the exercises, I found myself sitting in front of another student who had the habit of stroking his eyebrows, which weren't even bushy. He was talking about some personal issue, and I was supposed to practice being his coach. I had trouble listening. Had he recently trimmed his eyebrows? Maybe he went overboard with the trimmer? I wondered if my own eyebrows were bushy. I touched my brow, mirroring his gesture, then immediately put my hand down, not wanting to look like I was making fun of him. After a few minutes, he stopped talking and stared at me. I hadn't heard a word he'd said. I was supposed to ask him something intelligent, the kind of powerful question coaches ask, but my mind was blank.

"Wow, that was powerful," he said, stroking his eyebrow again. "You were so focused. I don't think anybody has ever listened to me so deeply."

A few minutes later, during group sharing, he raised his hand. The facilitator nodded at him.

"I just realized how powerful it is to be heard," he told the room. "Aidan didn't say much. He just listened. By the time I finished telling him about the problem I'm having at home, I knew what I needed to do."

Misha smiled. She launched into a talk about the power of deeply listening to another person, without judgment. She called it an act of healing. Other participants glanced at me as she spoke. Misha went through a list of things that get in the way of true listening. Like preparing what to say next or searching for ideas to fix the coachee's problem.

"Your greatest gift as a coach," she said, "is to create a space for your client to explore. Listening creates relationship. People become more connected. Trust grows. When you follow up with a powerful question, you further enable that exploration."

She paused then looked at me.

"Aidan... what did you notice about yourself, as the coach?"

Don't talk about the eyebrows. Say something profound.

"It felt like... he... needed someone to just listen."

"Exactly! Your instincts were spot on."

Another participant began sharing their experience of the exercise. I listened intently while stroking my eyebrow. Surely, there had to be more to this course than simply learning to stare silently while someone is talking.

Later in the day, Misha lectured on what she called trolls — limiting beliefs that get in our way, like I'm not good enough, or I can't tell the truth because I'll be judged, or my team can't operate without me... you get the idea.

"Mythical trolls are disruptive, and rarely helpful to human beings. When exposed to sunlight they burst or turn to stone. So, they live in dark places, like caves."

"In my case," I whispered to David, "it's not a cave, it's a massive, dark abyss."

He chuckled.

"Here is an example," Misha said. "It was once believed that the human body wasn't capable of running a mile in under four minutes," she said. "World-class athletes tried for decades, but failed, confirming the belief that it was impossible. Then, on May 6th, 1954, an athlete named Roger Bannister ran a mile in under four minutes. Forty-six days later another runner broke the four-minute mile, and a year later three other runners did it in a single race. How many of you know this story?"

More than half the room raised their hands.

"Before Roger Bannister," Misha continued, "what benefits do you think athletes got from believing it was impossible to run a mile in less than four minutes?"

There were lots of benefits in breaking the four-minute mile. But the benefits of believing it couldn't be broken? I couldn't see any.

"None," somebody said. "No benefits."

"Think about it," Misha said, "there's always a benefit to holding onto a belief. Can you see that?"

When nobody spoke up, she laughed.

"OK, let's look at this from another angle. Elephants. You might have seen elephants in Malaysia and Thailand tied to a stake with a thin rope. They could easily break free, but they don't. How come?"

"They don't believe they can," a woman in the front row said.

"Exactly. When they were babies, they were too little to break the rope. They eventually gave up trying. As adults, they continue to believe it's impossible to break free. They don't even try. Now... this brings us back to the same question again... what benefit do elephants get from believing they can't break free?"

"They don't have to try," David said.

"It's tiring to keep trying," she said, "when you already know you can't. It's easier to give up, isn't it?"

David must have been one of those good students in high school.

"Let's bring this closer to home," Misha said. "This morning, several of you spoke about wanting more work-life balance. Let's see a show of hands... how many of you would like better work-life balance?"

More than half raised their hands, including David. The whole idea of work-life balance had never resonated with me.

"Let's hear from a few of you who raised your hands. What problems are you having with work-life balance?"

A man complained he could never finish his days on time and could never have a full weekend without work.

A woman said she couldn't get to most of her meetings on time, because colleagues often scheduled back-to-back meetings with no buffer to get from one meeting room to the next.

Misha pointed at me. "Aidan, what did you tell me the other day about work-life balance?"

"Work-life balance wasn't an option when I was running my company."

"Why not? You said more than that..."

"Well... after a few years... I realized... I could be happily married, or I could continue building my company."

"How many people see work-life balance as a trade-off?"

Most hands went up.

"What I'm hearing," Misha said, "is that you want work-life balance but haven't been able to have it." She nodded along with many people in the room. "Now, right back to my earlier question... what benefit do you get from not having work-life balance?"

"There is no benefit!" David laughed.

"Of course, I want balance," a man in his sixties spoke up for the first time. "Who doesn't want to get home for dinner every night? We all want more work-life balance."

A younger man then spoke.

"I had to travel a week after my daughter was born," he said. "I missed out on her first few weeks of life. There is no benefit from the imbalance."

Others spoke of struggles with teenage children, suffering from their parent's late nights at work and busy weekends.

"I get it," Misha said. "I really do. I have no doubt you believe you want work-life balance. But stay with me here. Imagine this... one of your colleagues always manages to be on time for every single meeting. When you arrive at the meeting, she's already there. She even has her cup of coffee already, which you still need to get, right after setting your laptop down. Imagine she goes home in time for dinner. Every day. She gets all her work done before Friday evening, and her weekends are dedicated to her family. Imagine she always gets her monthly reports done on time. She delivers all her projects on schedule, without disrupting her personal life."

I looked around the room. There were a few thoughtful nods now.

"What would you say about such a person?"

"She doesn't have enough work," said a woman.

"She's not doing important work," said another.

"She must not be important," a man laughed, triggering giggles around the room.

After the laughter died down, there was silence. I understood what Misha was getting at.

Work-life balance meant not being valued and respected as an important member of the management team. One's relative importance was signalled precisely by being late to every meeting, working nights and weekends, and not having enough time for family. Based on their underlying belief systems, this was in direct conflict with work-life balance. The statement, "I want more personal time with my family," couldn't become reality. Underneath, a deep, powerful belief produced the actual behaviour of not having personal time.

"You want to have an important job," Misha said, "but you believe that requires sacrificing your family time. Are you getting this? Can you see how this insight can you help you become a better coach?"

I was starting to see it, yes.

"When you look at someone's actual results, not what someone says they want... you can help them discover their Trolls."

David raised his hand. Misha nodded at him.

"The four-minute mile," he said, "the benefit of believing you can't break it... is that you don't feel frustrated when you're just above four minutes. You can stop trying harder..."

Misha nodded and smiled at him.

"... and you don't have to change your beliefs," said the teacher's favourite.

"Bingo! That's probably the biggest benefit," Misha said. "You don't have to re-examine your beliefs. When you don't re-examine your beliefs, you don't have to change them."

Rationally, it made sense. I was ready to admit that I had an old piece of rope tying me to a stake, which I could easily break free of, if only I was aware of it. The problem though, was that I still couldn't see anything in my life that would correspond to trolls.

Misha pointed at a man sitting a few seats away from me.

"Albert," she said, "would you like to share what you told me on the break?"

Albert looked to his left and right, as if he might have been hoping she was talking to another Albert.

"Uh... OK." He put his right hand over his left shoulder, hugging himself halfway with just one arm. "I have always believed that I would die at around fifty... like all the men in my family."

"How old are you now?"

"Forty-two." He looked around at the people staring at him. "It's... something.... In my DNA..."

"You're afraid you'll end up like your father, or other men in your family?"

He nodded.

Misha turned to the rest of the room. "How many of you relate to this?"

A few hands went up. David's also.

I thought of my father, who grew old, alone, and bitter, in a little townhouse in a subdivision of hundreds of identical houses, where he spent hours, every day, watching Fox News and shouting at the TV, laughing at gays getting married, complaining about Western women becoming even more slutty than when he first came to America, and hating how immigrants come into the country illegally, unlike him. I couldn't see any comparisons with my life. And yet, the vision of the rotting eagle tugged at me. A memory grabbed me. Visiting him one year in autumn when the leaves were falling, wet and thick, in the cooler, rainier season just before the first snowfall. He let himself fall backwards into the pile of leaves. What struck me was how old his face looked. And he would have been... barely more than sixty.

"That's more than half the room," Misha said to Albert. "And how has that belief impacted you?"

"I... I can't imagine becoming old," he said. "I haven't been looking out for my health," Albert said in a low voice that would have been hard to hear if I hadn't been near him.

I remembered seeing him smoking outside on the sidewalk during a break; one of the few people to do so. And he definitely looked overweight.

"What does your doctor say?"

Albert looked at the ground. His face turned a bit red.

"I... I haven't seen a doctor," he said, "in over ten years."

Several people murmured around the room.

"That's a very cool belief to uncover," David whispered to me. He was excited by all this. "He's trying so hard to make his belief true. He's doing everything he can to die at fifty."

My father quit his job at the university soon after my mother left him. That happened when he was fifty, exactly my age now. He bought the townhouse next door for rental income and did some math tutoring for neighborhood high school kids. After a lifetime of travel, teaching university students and managing the mathematics department of various universities around the world, his world had shrunk to a townhouse with piles of dead leaves.

The vision of a rotting eagle was a wake-up call for change, a subconscious attempt to force me to embark on a journey of reinvention. I couldn't continue languishing under wet leaves, wasting away and ending up like my father. There was too much pain and suffering in that vision.

An old Buddhist saying, repeated several times in the manuscript, popped into my mind.

Pain is inevitable, suffering is optional.

"Now that you've started to see your trolls," Misha said, "what possibilities does this open for you?"

Albert pursed his lips as he thought.

"I realise... that I want to see my youngest daughter grow up and get married. She's nine. I would need to live to maybe sixty."

"What else?" Misha nodded and smiled.

"I... I need to see a doctor... for a checkup."

Several people clapped.

"My wife would be happy," he continued. "She's a doctor."

Several participants gasped. Even Misha looked surprised.

"What a perfect example of the power of our limiting beliefs," she said. "You have a doctor at home, and that's not enough to break free."

Misha asked if anybody else wanted to share. A woman who believed her perfectionist nature was critical to success, said that she had just discovered that the leader she admired most, Angela Merkel, had a long list of failures.

"I guess I don't need to be perfect," she said.

"How is perfectionism a problem?" Misha asked.

"I want to be seen as an empowering manager. But I feel I need to be involved in everything my people do."

"You don't trust them?"

"I do," she quickly said, while holding the microphone to her mouth as if she had more to say. "But... they make mistakes."

"And that confirms your belief that you need to be perfect. To make up for their imperfections."

"Exactly."

"Now that you're seeing your trolls... what new opportunities open up for you?"

"I... I used to believe... no, I still believe I'll become more empowering when I hire more experienced people. But maybe... I can learn to be more like Angela Merkel."

It struck me how amazingly creative and complex we are. We can hold countless contradictory beliefs in our minds at the same time, yet still function at high levels. I wondered how much further I could go if I put some of that baggage down.

I suddenly realised I was processing Misha's workshop through the insights I had read in *Five Steps To Joyful Wisdom*.

Seeing Into The Beautiful Abyss Of The Mind

Discomfort and resistance grow as opposing beliefs create internal conflict and we struggle to find meaning. This is the Beautiful Abyss Of The Mind. People in this stage of the Journey To Joyful Wisdom become aware of their contradictory beliefs. They notice their own highly creative attempts to avoid new information that contradicts their worldview, to avoid the pain and suffering of letting go of old beliefs.

Misha told us to pair up with a partner and share our biggest trolls.

"Let's expose your trolls to sunlight," she said.

David and I were already sitting side by side, so we turned our chairs to face each other.

David went first, which suited me since I was drawing a blank.

"I have to give my subordinates more autonomy," he said. "But any mistake they make would cause me to look bad. Or worse... incompetent."

He wrote that down in the notepad on his lap. I noticed Misha walking around the room, talking to pairs of participants. She looked like she was working her way toward our side of the room.

David looked at me with wide eyes.

"Oh, here's another," he said. "I have to manage very talented people... who know how to do things I don't really understand. If someone finds out my employees know more than me... I don't want to imagine what they could think. And if my employees find out... they won't respect me."

He wrote this down as well. There was nothing like this going on in my life. I had always been happy to hire people who knew more than me. David was having a flood of insights, and I was getting nothing.

"I have to delegate more... and STILL achieve the results I'm committed to," he went on. "But delegating means more work managing and supervising people... so how is that possible? That's a big troll."

He looked down at his notebook, then back at me.

"Wow," he laughed. "I have lots of trolls... they're so ugly."

"How are you guys coming along?" Misha stood in front of us.

"I've got so many trolls!" David looked like a kid with an over-flowing Halloween bag.

"How about you?" She looked at me.

"I can't really find any."

She gave me one of her looks that said, yeah, right.

"Here is one for you," she said. "An easy one. You say you want to be a professional coach, but you don't believe that's as highly regarded as being a tech entrepreneur. So, you're stuck in the middle, neither coach nor entrepreneur. You're not coaching, and you're not running a company anymore. You're teaching what you learned over the years. Which keeps you stuck in limbo."

She stepped away, without waiting for a response. I knew she was right. Rajiv had said pretty much the same thing.

"Ouch," David said.

Clearly, the course was more about inner work than learning actual coaching skills. While I expected to explore some of my limiting beliefs, I didn't think the course would go so deep.

"The mind creates the abyss, the heart crosses it."
— Sri Nisargadatta Maharaj
Awareness leads to a point of no turning back, a dark night of

the soul, where it becomes evident deep personal transformation can no longer be avoided. Eventually, shame gives way to a joy-filled sense of simply being human with flaws like all other human beings. When the distinction between pain and suffering is understood, when internal conflict is seen as a sign of being alive, then we are ready to move to step three of the Journey To Joyful Wisdom.

David had to leave right after the workshop. I decided to stay back to see Misha. The way she talked about internal conflicting beliefs made me think she had read the manuscript, and maybe even knew the writer.

"MacRitchie tomorrow morning," David said, referring to his earlier agreement to join Matt and I for our weekly rainforest walk.

"Absolutely."

"Also... Rajiv will be joining us."

"That's great! I need to make things better with him."

"Don't worry," David smiled. "You're fine."

I waited for several participants to finish talking to Misha. When the last person left, I helped her put away her markers, Blu-tack and unused flip chart paper.

"Have you seen this?" I handed her the manuscript.

"*Five steps to joyful wisdom,*" she read the title out loud, then shook her head.

"It's... really interesting. I'm not into religious literature, but this isn't really religious."

She turned the manuscript over to read the back.

"Everything you talked about today is part of the second chapter."

Misha glanced at me, then opened it.

"Seeing into the beautiful abyss of the mind?"

"That's it."

She barely read it before handing the manuscript back.

"Cognitive dissonance was first written about in the 1950s. It's been around a long time, but it's not ancient wisdom."

How could she be so sure cognitive dissonance hadn't been discovered much earlier?

"You're sure you haven't heard of it?"

She shook her head.

"I wanted to find the author, but there's no name anywhere."

"Google?"

"I typed in the title and a bunch of key phrases. There were thousands of similar hits, but not this particular text."

"Why would someone print something like this and leave it anonymous?"

"That's what I was wondering. It doesn't make sense."

"It really touched you."

"Yeah... I guess it did. There's so much here that fits my life right now."

She nodded her head in her coaching way, which made it hard not to talk.

"The stuff I'm going through... seems so heavy... but maybe it doesn't need to be. The writer describes a painful process in an almost joyful way. It's as if he or she or they or whatever... have reached a point where inner growth and transformation is joyful."

"Wow."

"I want some of that."

"I get it."

"Plus, I finally signed up for your coaching program after I read it."

"Well, that's a good thing!" She laughed.

"I'll get you a copy when I go back to the Indian restaurant where I found it. I'll ask them if they know the writer."

She stared at me with a knowing smile.

"What?"

"You're on a search for enlightenment," she grinned.

"I... I don't... well, maybe."

"You're looking for a guru."

It did sound silly. I folded the manuscript and put it in my pocket.

"Wait, let me see it again."

I handed the manuscript to her.

"The beautiful abyss of the mind," her eyes darted across the page. "That does sound very familiar. That's where all the trolls live."

"Exactly."

"What a curious way to describe a dark cave filled with monsters."

"Isn't it? I love it!"

She kept reading.

"Keep it," I said.

"Are you sure?"

"I'll get another one."

The restaurant was on my way home, if I went in a big circle to get to my place. When I got there, it was already full for dinner. A couple families waited outside for a table. The evening crowd was very different from what I was used to. More families, instead of executives and other workers having a quick lunch before going back to work.

"We're full," said the cashier. "How many will you be?"

"I just wanted to pick up..." I reached for a booklet next to the cash register, "one of these."

Several people pushed up in front of me to pay, so I stepped aside. The cashier then called in the family waiting closest to the door and pointed at the newly freed up table. I waited for him to finish. A waiter shouted something from the back of the room. The cashier responded with a head bob. Then he disappeared. Several more people were at the cash register now, waiting for him to return. Finally, he was back. I tried to keep out of the way as people asked me if I was waiting to pay. I started to realise this wasn't a good time to chat. But I was already here.

"Why are you waiting? Did you change your mind?"

"No."

"I can get you a table for one person." He pointed at a tiny spot tucked behind the refrigerated display unit filled with Indian pastries.

"I just want to ask you..."

He was busy again, talking to people who seemed to be regular patrons.

After he finished ringing up a customer's order, there was a pause. No customers waiting. I jumped in.

"Where did you get these?" I pointed at the stack of booklets.

"I don't know." Then he called out to a waiter, holding up a booklet.

The waiter answered him.

"Someone left them here in the morning."

"You don't know who?"

He shook his head.

"Don't know, man. Try Google."

I was about to say I already did, but a customer was waiting.

"I'm sorry. Yes. I'll... I'll try that. Thank you." I reached for more booklets. "May I?"

He nodded.

I took several, with the vague intention of giving them to David and Rajiv in the morning.

Becoming Comfortable Feeling Uncomfortable

The entrance to the MacRitchie Nature Trail serves as a portal to a tropical rainforest filled with long-tailed macaque monkeys, wild chickens, monitor lizards, flying lemurs and countless tropical birds. I could feel the coolness of the jungle from the taxi stand where Matt and I waited for David and Rajiv. It was a cloudy morning, which would make the walk even nicer.

I was glad when David told me he had invited Rajiv to join us. I hadn't spoken to Rajiv since the restaurant and was looking forward to clearing things up. Today, we would go on a hike as friends. It would be an informal outing with no agenda.

"What do your friends look like?" Matt peered through his binoculars at the cars coming toward the taxi stand.

"An Indian and a European."

"What part of India?"

"I don't know," I laughed. "The European man is from France. Mediterranean looking."

"I think today is the day we see the eagle," Matt said.

"I hope you're right."

He was in a good mood. I loved feeling useful as something of a father figure.

"There's a taxi with one guy in it," Matt spoke while squinting through the binoculars. "He's by himself."

Sure enough, a taxi arrived with David in the back, and no Rajiv.

"Rajiv had to go to Mumbai," David said as he got out.

"Another accident?"

"He didn't say. But that's what I thought too. All he said was that he had to leave this morning, unexpectedly."

"I can't imagine what he's going through."

Had I completely messed up my relationship with Rajiv before I even got to know him?

"And this is Matt," I said, "Misha's boy."

"I saw you coming before he did," Matt said.

David laughed. "How did you know it was me?"

"Zeiss lenses." Matt held out his binoculars. "Eight times magnification. And Aidan described you well. He said you looked Arab."

"Mediterranean looking!" I laughed. "I didn't say Arab."

David laughed.

We stepped into the shade of the thick jungle canopy. Matt walked ahead of us, scanning the treetops and the sky. He was still looking for the big, male White Bellied Sea Eagle.

"I was looking forward to seeing Rajiv," I said.

"Do you think it's going to rain?"

The clouds didn't look too dark.

"Maybe later in the day."

"I wouldn't want to be stuck here in a downpour," David said.

The rain didn't bother me. I was more worried about lightning.

Matt seemed to be in a good mood. He was very focused on his search for the eagle.

Monkeys foraged and played in the trees, mostly oblivious to our presence, except for a very curious juvenile who followed us a few steps before getting scolded by an adult. The dirt at the edges of the trail had recently been dug up, the work of wild boars that tended to stay deeper in the jungle during the day.

Matt was ahead of us, uninterested in our conversation, so we shifted to French. David talked rapid fire about using his new coaching techniques at work. A young manager wanted to know how to get better at her job.

"I asked her what kind of manager she wanted to be. She immediately said inspiring. Then I did what you do. I asked her how she would rate herself as an inspiring manager."

A wild rooster crowed nearby. When I looked toward the sound, I saw a colourful red and black rooster proudly watching over two hens scratching at the dirt.

"It's so awesome," I said, "to have all this nature in the middle of a big city."

David glanced at the rooster briefly before getting back to his story.

"She said three out of ten. So, I asked the next question... what level would you like to get to and by when?"

We were going up a hill now, causing him to take a breath.

"She said it would take a long time to become inspiring. Maybe ten or fifteen years. Just to get to six or seven. Her Troll was that she needed lots more experience."

As I listened to him, I was also looking out for wild boar. I had seen several before, but not often. The dirt dug up near the path looked fresh. Perhaps we would see one today.

"And then... here is the cool part... I didn't mention it, but she's pregnant. She'll be going on maternity leave in a few weeks. So, I asked her..."

"Look," I tapped him on the shoulder and pointed at a monitor lizard walking slowly across the path ahead of us. We slowed down to let the lizard go peacefully.

"I asked her... how long will it take you to become the best mother you can be. Your ten out of ten. Totally loving, dedicated... and... inspiring."

David was walking almost sideways now, facing me while talking, with his arms waving in wide gestures. He reminded me of a crab scurrying across a beach, waving its claws.

"What did she say?"

He had a big smile.

"The look on her face... she laughed and was like... OH!"

David was glowing. His mouth was open, as if he was mimicking the woman's aha moment.

"She was already getting it, but I went on. I said, imagine saying to your new-born child... this is going to sound silly... on a scale of one to ten, my love for you is around a seven. There's always room for improvement, and nobody can be a perfect ten, right? I look forward to loving you more, as I gradually learn to be a parent, and as we get to know each other over the years."

He was bouncing as he walked.

"She got it. Right then. She said she would immediately be the best mother she could be. I told her... but... you don't have any experience being a mother. Don't you need five or ten years' experience? She laughed and said, I got it, I got it."

He stopped walking. I stopped too and faced him. His eyes glistened and sparkled.

"I don't ever remember," he said in a lower, more deliberate voice, "anytime in my life... feeling more valuable... than I did in that moment."

There was a look of peace and serenity in his face. Not just in his face, it was also in the relaxed way he carried himself at this moment. I realised he often had an edgy look, like he was tensed up. But that was gone. He might even have been standing taller.

"You seem a lot lighter," I said.

"That's it. So much lightness."

We continued walking. He was quiet now. I let him be in whatever reflections and processing he was going through. David just started to learn how to coach, and already he was coaching people in a way that seemed to be producing awesome results. I had been doing this longer, but I couldn't think of a moment similar to what David just experienced.

"The other day," he said in English, since Matt had slowed down enough for us to catch up to him, "I saw a bluish-black bird around here. I don't know what it was. But it reminded me of Australian Lyrebirds."

"Did you notice the tail?" Matt stared intently at David.

"The tail was... strange."

"Did the tail look like two long wires with a feather at the end of each?"

"Yeah, exactly."

"They remind me of Lyrebirds too," I said. I couldn't name or recognize most birds. But this one stood out.

"What you saw was a Greater Racket-tailed Drongo," Matt said.

"A Drongo?"

"A Greater Racket-tailed Drongo. Its tail is the product of evolution. Actually, the whole bird is."

"Wow... you know birds."

"Matt is like a walking encyclopedia on many things."

"You know," David said, "after I saw that bird with the strange tail... I couldn't get David Attenborough's voice out of my head."

We continued walking. When Matt was a bit further ahead, we could hear him whistling, imitating bird songs. I couldn't tell the difference between actual bird songs and Matt's whistling.

"He seems happy," David whispered in French. "Why is Misha so worried?"

"Time together outdoors is good for him. The psychiatrist recommended it. He's usually happy when we're out together."

"You're like a father and son."

"It does feel like that sometimes. Misha is busier than I am. So, it's often just Matt and I, out for these walks."

I didn't want to tell David that there was always a potential outburst lurking beneath Matt's apparent peacefulness. There was always the fear that the next outburst would be a big one, like when he heard about the dead eagle family and started hyperventilating so hard that his legs went numb, and he fainted.

"I couldn't stay in Singapore very long without this bit of jungle," I said.

"You crave connection."

I looked at him.

"Yeah," he said. "It's all about connection. You live in one of the world's most modern and culturally diverse cities, because you crave connection with other people like you. And you crave connection with nature too. I can't imagine you being anywhere else in the world."

"Sometimes I can imagine this city in twenty or thirty years," I said. "Electric cars everywhere. Even more public transportation. And boulevards converted back to jungle. I can imagine two or three big bands of jungle from one side of the island to the other. I call them Jungle Wildlife Corridors. JWC for short. Everybody loves acronyms so much."

"I'll be back in France, by then. But I'll think back to this day when I see pictures of Singapore in the news, with those wildlife boulevards."

"Jungle Wildlife Corridors. That's what I think they'll be called."

"Yeah that," he laughed.

When we got back to the main road, David waved down a cab.

"Matt and I are going to continue our walk. We need to check the old eagle's nest, deeper in the rainforest."

"You should call Rajiv," David said as the cab came to a stop.

"Is he expecting me to call?"

"I didn't tell you..."

He was turning red. Was he embarrassed, or was that from our walk?

"I only told Rajiv last night that we were meeting you here today."

"He thought it would be just you two?"

David nodded.

"Ah. So..."

"Maybe he changed his mind this morning..."

"Because he didn't want to see me."

David sighed.

"He's not used to being challenged," he said. "And he's suffering from the pressure at work."

"I get that."

"Give him a call."

I nodded.

David stepped into the cab and drove off. I felt lightheaded, a bit nauseous. Who was I to suggest Rajiv wasn't one hundred percent committed to safety? I wasn't living his life. I knew nothing about what it felt like being in his shoes.

Matt and I went down a different path, cutting through the rainforest, towards a hill overlooking the eagle's nest. The thick growth made it difficult to keep up with Matt. I ran into a thorny vine that scratched my chest and arms and stuck to my shirt. Pulling it off with my hand caused the thorn pricks to twist deeper into my palm. I finally got the vine off me, but my arm was throbbing in pain. Somehow, my left thigh had caught it as well, leaving small rivulets of blood dripping down my leg.

When we got to a lookout point where we could see the nest from above, Matt looked through his binoculars without moving, for what seemed like a few minutes. I knew he wouldn't see anything. The eagle was probably dead, but neither Misha nor I were going to tell Matt.

A few raindrops started to fall.

"Do you see anything?"

Matt was silent.

I took a deep breath, smelling the shift in the air. A storm was definitely brewing.

"We should probably start heading back now."

Matt continued peering through his binoculars. Then he put them down, turned around, and walked past me.

"We'll have to go faster," he picked up his pace, almost jogging now. "Rain is coming. Probably lightening too."

The rain caused the scratches to burn. As I ran to keep up with Matt, the pain in my leg turned into a sharp throbbing burn. Maybe I could stop and let the rain wash off whatever was causing the stinging. But I couldn't let Matt go on his own.

The old saying from the manuscript popped into my head again.

Pain is inevitable, suffering is optional.

Along with the phrase, an almost thirty-year-old memory appeared.

"Pain is inevitable, suffering is optional." Those words were spoken by the paediatrician to my wife, who was about to deliver our baby.

Back then, Boulder, Colorado still had a hippie town vibe. There was a strong Buddhist influence with the Naropa Institute just a few blocks away from the hospital. I would learn years later that the phrase on pain and suffering came from the mindfulness world. The doctor's advice fit the time and place and echoed decades into the future, reaching me here in a Singaporean jungle.

What was the doctor's name? Julie something. I remember how she kept telling my wife to breathe through the contractions, ride the pain, stop resisting the contractions.

"Resistance only brings suffering." I said the words out loud as soon as they came back to me.

Thinking back to that hospital delivery room, I remembered not knowing what to do. The doctor was busy doing doctor stuff, a nurse ran in and out of the room doing her things, and I just stood there letting my wife squeeze my hand while she screamed, pushed, and cried. I felt useless. I needed to do something, fix something, reduce the pain or at least take her mind off it.

The doctor kept repeating the same three words.

"Breathe! Push! Now!"

I somehow got the idea I too could tell my wife what to do. I started repeating the same words, in the same authoritative voice as the doctor.

"Breathe! Push! Now!"

This was not appreciated. My wife squeezed my hand even harder and shouted at me in French to shut up, which I did. So, I went back to just being there, not trying to do anything.

The memory was funny now. At the time I was embarrassed.

Pain is inevitable, suffering is optional. I understood this better now than I did back then. Pain is the actual difficult event, usually external, that directly causes discomfort — something that is mainly outside our control. Like getting wrapped up in a thorn bush. Or things others do, like the partner who cheated on you, corporate management cutting costs and your job, or the cancer or dementia that's stealing a loved one away. Suffering is how we interpret and process the event. It's something we do to ourselves through our thoughts, beliefs, and attitudes. Suffering is the stuff that is internally generated, from within your mind. All the judgments you have about the situation. The ways you resist or fight it, causing you to become angry and feel victimised, to the point of focusing on the pain so hard that the rest of your awareness shrinks to encompass very little more than the pain. I knew all this. I knew that scientists have been able to show that suffering represents around half of the discomfort that comes with pain. They did this by exploring how mindfulness reduces the perceived intensity and experience of pain, the suffering part, by helping us become less attached to our thoughts, beliefs, and stories. It helps us let go of our Trolls.

I knew all this. But I wasn't applying it to my life.

Looking at my life now — what part of my current experience was due to pain, and what part was due to suffering? What part of my professional transformation was due to the actual discomfort of change, the normal process of learning something new? And what part was due to stuff internally generated within my mind, making the pain worse than it needed to be?

Simply asking the question helped my mind open up and relax. I could instantly realise I was creating suffering for myself. The clenching loosened. There was a sense of the mind settling, ever so slightly. When I had done this before, I had always found that my mind gradually let go of the suffering, without even needing to rationally understand everything.

A wild boar jumped across the path in front of us, followed by three piglets, instantly forcing me to snap out of my thoughts. As we walked by, I glanced toward the trees they had disappeared into, and briefly caught a glimpse of a piglet with its distinctive black-and-white-striped back.

That was when the rain really started to fall. The low, black clouds suggested there was lots more coming. The sky grumbled in the distance; a long, deep, rumbling. I had to get Matt out of the jungle, immediately.

"We need to speed up," I said.

Matt ran next to me, awkwardly holding his binoculars in his hands so they wouldn't bounce against his chest. This prevented him from running quickly.

Then, a sharp clap of thunder, followed moments later by a bright flash of lightning, jagged and splintering through the sky.

"Two seconds," Matt said. "That means it's less than a kilometre away."

Rain poured. The trail became a gully. My shirt and shorts stuck to my body, soaked. My running shoes squelched.

I tried to remember what we were supposed to do in a lightning storm. Were we too close to the trees? Was it better to be running under the trees than in a clearing? How far was the park entrance shelter near the parking lot? I recognised a bend in the trail. One and a half more kilometres. Running through muddy water, that would take us at least fifteen minutes.

My breathing became difficult, and my heart was beating in my ears. I couldn't keep running this fast.

What part of this is pain, and what part is suffering?

The question boomed in my head. I realised there wasn't much pain... yet. I hadn't tripped and fallen, I hadn't gotten hit by lightning, and I hadn't stepped on a snake hiding under the muddy water (one of my big irrational fears in this situation). Everything I was experiencing in this moment was suffering due to the fears and images and ruminating that my mind had locked onto.

Then another flash of lightning, followed almost immediately by thunder and the sound of a tree splitting. At least, that's what I imagine had just happened.

Matt shrieked, and I probably did too.

What part of this is pain, and what part is suffering?

I needed to focus on getting out of the jungle. I reminded myself that I knew the path well. In ten minutes, I would be safe. My shoes were designed for trails. They were soaked but held their grip. I tried to glance at Matt's shoes, but they were covered in mud.

Moments later, I could see the parking lot, and the building next to it with water fountains and toilets and a big map of the park. We had been closer to the entrance than I thought. A dozen people or more stood in the shelter, out of the rain, where we quickly joined them.

"You're bleeding," Matt said.

"I'll be fine. The rain is good."

I went into the bathroom to wash my arms and leg with soap.

Back out under the shelter again with Matt, the rain continued just as hard. I texted Misha to let her know we were both fine but soaked. I thought of calling Rajiv while waiting, since there wasn't much else to do. I wondered if the heavy beating on the roof would make it difficult to talk. I texted him instead.

Rajiv, sorry we missed you this morning. I'd love to meet up for a coffee when you're back.

After a couple minutes waiting for a response, I started to think it would have been better to call. Then my phone dinged.

Sorry, can't talk. I'm out of town.

Yes, I knew that.

When will you be back?

A minute went by, then a few more.

How presumptuous of me to think I could coach someone dealing with workplace fatalities. Rajiv was struggling with life and death situations, and there I was pretending to be able to coach him. If I could go back just a short while in time to that lunch with the Nomads, I would have said, *Sorry Rajiv, but I can't coach you.* That would have been the honest truth.

Had I finally reached a point in my life where I could no longer fake my way? Throughout my career, I had gotten away with taking on new, bigger roles that I wasn't qualified for. I had always been lucky. I could fake my way into a role, like CEO, that I wasn't fit for, then gradually grow into it without getting caught. Was my luck running out?

Then that inner voice again — calm and accepting.

What part of this is pain, and what part is suffering?

I realised that what I was experiencing in this moment was mostly suffering, due to my own thoughts. The realisation pulled me back from the edge of the dark place I was falling into.

The rain stopped. I took Matt back to his place. Misha's helper, Gloria, made pizza, which we ate while listening to Matt talk about how fast we ran, how close the lightening was, and how the eagle nest was still empty, but he was sure he saw fresh feathers in the nest. I didn't think the binoculars were powerful enough to tell if a feather is fresh, but I didn't say anything.

After dinner, Matt went to his room to play video games, and Misha and I finished a bottle of wine. Misha opened her laptop.

"I wanted to get your opinion on something." She typed at the keyboard, then turned the laptop to show me a LinkedIn profile of a woman. "She's new at work. I think she's really interesting."

My curiosity turned to annoyance. I pushed the laptop back toward her.

"Come on," she said. "Just take a look. She's American... she's lived in France, like you, and Italy. And look at all the connections she has! People like her!"

"I'm not interested."

"Aw, come on. Just take a look."

"Only you can make dating feel like a professional hiring process."

Misha sighed.

"I'm really not interested."

"But why?"

"Blind dates don't turn out well. I don't have the energy for that."

"It's been... what, half a year? Things might be different."

"I've been on dates."

"How long ago? Six months?"

"More recently than that."

"Five months?"

I sighed and finished my wine.

"OK, then at least go Salsa dancing with me."

I hadn't been back to Salsa since dropping out from the classes Misha had paid for.

"It was painful," I said.

"You didn't give it enough time."

"I couldn't ever find the one beat..."

"You were learning."

"Look, I'll pay you back."

"It was a gift. I don't want the money back."

I got up to leave.

"It would do you so much good."

"Misha, I have two left feet. And no class can fix that."

Matt appeared in the living room, grinning, and almost bouncing.

"I found him!"

Misha looked up at him and smiled, catching his excitement.

"Who?"

"Dad!"

"What?" Her eyes bulged. She looked as if someone had punched her. "Your dad?"

"Online. It was easy. You didn't try hard enough."

"You... What?"

"He wants to see me!"

Now he really was bouncing foot to foot.

"You're not..."

"I'm baggage here."

He was calm, as if he'd thought about it a long time. How did he even find his father? How long had they been talking? What's this about baggage?

"But... You don't even know him."

"He said he'd like me to come see him."

"When..."

"He'll get back to me in a day or two."

"No, I mean, when did you find him? How?"

"Google. Then I emailed him."

Why was he so calm?

"You don't know him," she said. "You can't go live with him!"

"Yes, I can."

"No, you can't. When you're eighteen, you can do what you want."

Matt glared at her and crossed his arms. He grunted something that sounded like "whatever" condensed into a single gruff syllable, then turned and stomped off toward his room, slamming his bedroom door, not once, but twice.

Misha looked at me with her mouth wide open. "What the hell was that?"

I shook my head.

"I didn't think it was that easy to find someone," she said.

"It's not."

"Damn! Why is everything so difficult? The asshole left when Matt was a baby. He's never been around... and now he's the saviour? And I'm the bad guy?"

I sighed, not sure what to say.

"Why do teenage boys crave a father figure?" Her mouth was still open.

"He said baggage... what's that about?"

She shook her head. "No idea."

A shout came from Matt's room, in his teenage boy becoming man voice, a long, angry, "FUCK!"

Misha and I looked at each other.

"Let me go talk to him," I said.

"No! Stay out of it."

"I can help."

"Aidan, don't!"

"I just want to help. We had a good time on our walk."

"Stop trying to fix things."

"I'm not..."

"Stop, Aidan."

"If he needs a male figure... I'm here, now! I can help."

"I don't need your help! I don't need anyone's help! I'll handle this! I'm his mother!"

It was no use arguing with her when she was this determined. I finished my glass of wine, gave her a hug, and left.

I walked up the two flights of stairs to my place and noticed a missed call from a number I didn't recognise. I dialled the number.

"Aidan," said a woman's voice. "It's Joanna."

"Joanna?"

"From the Nomads."

"Oh, right!"

"I'm about to go into a meeting. But I need to see you. Can you do lunch tomorrow?"

She sounded formal, very business-like.

"Lunch is good."

Pain And Suffering

Recall a situation or person causing you to experience painful emotions. What feelings come to mind? Does the experience trigger feelings of being overwhelmed or pressured? Perhaps there is a sense of helplessness or fear. Is there sadness? Maybe there is anger, frustration, or bitterness. Often there is a mix of emotions. Some of the deeper ones lurk in the shadows, hiding behind other emotions that appear more readily.

Where do you feel these emotions in your body? Close your eyes and feel into the pain. Is there a tightness somewhere? A clenching? Sometimes the mind is so focused on the pain that we have difficulty experiencing anything else. Is it instead a generalised feeling, spread out and difficult to pinpoint?

Now ask yourself... if pain is inevitable and suffering optional... what part of my experience is due to actual pain, and what part is due to suffering?

Can you engage with the pain just as it is? Instead of trying to fix it, or make it go away... can you approach it with curiosity, kindness, and self-compassion? You are a human being experiencing all that living human beings experience. Can you allow the pain to exist within you?

What part of this experience is pain, and what part is suffering?

You don't need to find an answer. Simply asking the question to yourself begins to tease the two apart. The question is in fact a statement, a declaration to your subconscious that part of the unpleasant experience is created through your own thoughts and beliefs. It does not need to be.

What part of this experience is pain, and what part is suffering?

Have you noticed a sense of possessiveness? MY back pain, my migraines, my cancer, my divorce, my failed startup, my addiction, my anger management issues. The pain becomes part of our identity. By bringing a kind and mindful attention to both the pain and our resistance to it, the identification can dissolve. If you notice yourself saying

MY pain, can you try to think of it as THE pain instead?

What can I let go of?

If you were to stop resisting the pain, what must you let go of? You might find that you want to let go of self-judgment, or judgment of another. Or maybe you've become hooked on telling your story from the point of view of someone who has been wronged, or unfairly treated. Perhaps you need to let go of an assessment you might be holding onto regarding another person. Whatever it is, you can explore what it would feel like if you were to let go of that.

You don't need to actually let go; you're simply exploring what letting go feels like.

Transcendence Through Compassion

When I was running my company, people were almost never late for meetings. Either because they had flown to the south of France specifically for meetings at my office, or I had flown somewhere to see them. Yet, there I was, sitting in my Indian restaurant sipping a cup of masala tea, waiting for Joanna. She was over thirty minutes late and hadn't answered my text messages.

Amit the waiter stopped at my table after delivering a couple trays to two men sitting near me. He raised his eyes and shrugged.

"Not here yet," I said.

"Your friend is late."

"Yes, a bit."

He pointed at my empty glass of water. I nodded.

"But I have a question," I pulled out a booklet. "Have you seen this?"

He took it from me and looked at the front and back.

"They're at the counter," he said, "next to the door."

"Do you know who put them there?"

He shook his head.

"I want to find the writer."

Amit looked at the cover again, then handed it back at me.

"Did you try Google?"

"Yes. Nothing."

He shrugged and was gone again.

Where was Joanna? Had she flown off somewhere suddenly and forgotten to cancel lunch? Like Rajiv?

The men at the table next to me, an Indian and an Australian, were talking about an event that had been in the news that morning. A dog was swallowed by a python, not far from where David, Matt and I had been walking.

"Up in the Northern Territory," the Australian said, "crocodiles sometimes swallow dogs. I heard of a Mastiff taken by a six-meter croc. Swallowed in one bite."

"That's a big dog," his friend said.

"Mate, it was over in a couple seconds."

I tried to tune the men out as they talked about dogs and pythons and crocodiles. Then the Australian said something that caught my attention.

"I've learned so much from every one of my pups. Forgive and forget. Don't hold a grudge. Leave the past in the past."

"Play whenever you can."

"Exactly! Why be sad when you're alive and can play?"

"Dogs are the best teachers ever."

"I've learned more from my dogs than any teacher I ever had!"

There was a pause.

"I couldn't imagine losing a dog like that," the Australian said.

My phone buzzed. It was Joanna.

"I'm so sorry. I'm still stuck in a meeting with my CEO."

"No worries."

"I'm so embarrassed..."

"I'm just glad you're still in town."

"Ugh... I never do this."

"Hey, your CEO is important."

"Coffee later? I really want to tell you what happened."

What happened with what?

"I'm free," I said.

"Can you meet me at a place next to my office? I'll text you."

"I'll be there."

The restaurant had filled up quickly for lunch and was now emptying out. I waved at Amit. He nodded, knowing what I wanted.

Moments later, the Thali tray was in front of me, with a piece of roti prata still steaming.

When I finished eating, the restaurant was much quieter. Amit stood at my table, looking like he wanted to talk. This was unusual. He was usually gone by the time the lunch rush was over.

"Did you hear what the men next to you were talking about? The python?"

I nodded.

"Sometimes in India, pythons also eat dogs. Also, goats, chickens."

I thought a joke was coming. But Amit was somber.

"When I was a boy," Amit said, "I broke a vase that my mother loved. When My father came to see what happened, I blamed it on my dog, Dosa. My father was furious. He ran out of the house looking for him. I ran after him, feeling shameful for lying and hoping he wouldn't hurt Dosa."

Amit paused a moment. I pointed at the chair in front of me. He sat down.

"I loved that dog. His name was Dosa, because he was the color of... well, dosa bread."

Amit glanced down at the table, as if he was remembering.

"We found a python in the garden, trying to swallow poor Dosa. My father screamed and kicked the snake until it let go and slithered away."

"Was Dosa OK?"

"It was too late." Amit frowned. "I wanted Dosa to get up and shake it all off. But he didn't."

In that moment, as he paused, reliving an event from many years earlier, it was easy to imagine Amit as a boy.

"I'm sure my father knew I broke the vase. But we never talked about it. He knew I was suffering enough shame. If I had only gone out to play with Dosa... instead of playing with my ball in the living room. The snake wouldn't have caught Dosa. And I would not have broken the vase."

A look of boyhood shame flashed across Amit's face. Teenage Amit was sitting across the table from me.

"Later, my father repaired the vase with gold paste, the way he repaired other broken pieces of pottery. He said it was to honour the cracks. I remember his words. Every living being has cracks, he said. Like the vase. Either we hide them and become shameful of our flaws, or we celebrate them."

"Isn't that a... Japanese thing?"

"He loved Japanese art."

Singapore was filled was fascinating people like Amit, a waiter in a small restaurant in Little India, whose father practiced a form of Japanese art.

"Your father sounds like a very wise man."

"My father was my biggest teacher. Like all fathers, right?"

I tried to remember similar memories with my father, but nothing came to mind.

"My father was a university professor," I said, "mathematics."

As a boy, I frequently went to the university with him. I had seen him interact with other professors, who all clearly respected him. I watched him teach at the front of a class of at least a hundred students. I saw students (grown men to me) approach him after class asking questions, drinking up his answers like dry, grateful sponges.

Education was everything to my father. Being at the top of his class took him from Morocco to California and then universities around the world. Education was his escape to a better life. And he demanded that of his only child. Grades were everything. I dreaded bringing home a report card because there would always be something to criticise. So, in defiance, I slacked. Mediocre grades were my way of rebelling. Once, when my grades were particularly bad, he flew into a rage and smashed my guitar. He later helped pay for a new one, but the damage was done. I wished I could find warm memories similar to those Amit was sharing.

"... and that's why, Dosa was also my teacher," Amit had been speaking but I only caught the end of what he was saying. "I learned so much from that dog, just like they were saying." He nodded toward the now empty table next to mine. "Funny thing though... I only became aware of that after he was gone."

Amit appeared deep in thought. It wouldn't have been right to interrupt his thoughts. The stillness was perfect, almost sacred. My heart felt big, full, and tender. There was no need to teach or give advice. The stillness was far more valuable than any piece of advice I could possibly give.

"Don't throw away a broken vase," he said after a long pause. "Celebrate the breaks and imperfections with gold. The cracks are signs of age, resilience, and wisdom."

"What beautiful memories."

He paused again. The moment floated on still calmness. Then he left to clear a table.

Thinking of my father, something suddenly clicked, and I could see, clear as day, one of my biggest trolls. I knew what I was grappling with. It had always been right there in front of me, but I hadn't seen it. It had to do with the respect my father enjoyed from his students and colleagues. I realised I had always craved that kind of respect.

Teaching is the most valuable and honourable profession.

I don't think my father actually said those words, but I had enough evidence as a boy to put that belief together and make it hard as fact.

If people want to learn from me, then I am valuable and worthy of respect.

I have often noticed how speaking to a large audience made me wonder if I was like my father when he taught. Now it was all clear — I wanted to be like him and at the same time hated being like him. I was fighting with myself.

I felt light now. Naming the belief took its power away. I knew it was just a boy's belief. It didn't have to be real anymore. Whispering the belief to myself caused it to crumble. Like turning to face a shadowy, mysterious pursuer in a nightmare, instantly causing the dark thing to fade away.

If people want to learn from me, then I am valuable and worthy of respect.

Now, half a century later, I had discovered a limiting belief acquired as a boy, which was still driving me today and preventing me from growing further.

"I have had one single spiritual goal my entire life," Amit said, pulling me out of my thoughts. "I learned this from Dosa. It is to be gentle with myself and others. If I can't be kind with myself, how can I be kind to others? If I have a philosophy, it is transcendence through compassion."

"What a wonderful gift from Dosa. I am very happy to have met Dosa today. Thank you for that."

"You're right. Dosa is still alive." He smiled and put his hand on his heart.

Moments later, I watched Amit leave the restaurant. He was probably heading off to his other job.

When I paid my bill, I asked the cashier about the booklet.

"Try the temple," she said.

"The temple?"

"They often distribute flyers like this."

The booklet did look something like a flyer or pamphlet announcing religious activities in Hindu temples. Perhaps they were making some of their teachings more secular.

"Which temple?"

"Try the big temple up the road. Sri Veeramakaliamman."

"Sri..."

"The colourful one on Serangoon Road."

I rushed to the temple. It wouldn't take long; I could still meet Joanna on time.

The temple was empty, other than a few tourists and someone praying to a sculpture of the Hindu goddess Kali. It was a black sculpture, not Kali's usual blue. Black, just like the mysterious Sara-la-Kali, the patron saint of Gypsies, hidden in a crypt under an old church, ten thousand kilometres away, in a small town very close to where I lived for almost twenty years, where I started my company, and raised my daughter. Goosebumps tickled the back of my neck. I was in the right place; I was sure of it.

"This is our mother, Kali," a woman I hadn't noticed before was standing next to me.

"Yes, I recognize her. Do you work here?"

"Oh no. I saw you in devotion."

"I wasn't... yeah... I like... she's special to me."

"And to all of us. This is her home."

"Do you know if there is someone who works here?"

"Is Kali known in your world?"

What is my world? The woman looked sincerely curious.

"There is a town in France," I skipped the name of the town, Saintes-Maries-de-la-Mer, always difficult to explain to non-French speakers, "where every year in May... the 24th of May, to be exact... Gypsies come on a pilgrimage from all over Europe. They have their own version of Kali, that they take out on a platform, into the sea."

Chantal, Val and I would watch the procession together from a seaside cafe, almost every year.

"In the sea? Just like we do?"

"With flowers and everything." I nodded.

"Are they Hindu?"

"They are Catholic, and other religions. But originally, they came from India."

This was Chantal's academic expertise. My words would never do justice to my wife's anthropological research. All those years listening to Chantal speak about her favorite topic gave me a unique view of Kali. Chantal had a special interest in the spread of Kali mythology around the world and wrote a seminal paper on Kali's transformation from Hindu goddess to Gypsy saint, as a way of exploring the emergence of informal cultural expressive forms across time and place, bridging tradition with modernity.

"Kali represents change and transformation," the woman said.

I nodded. Chantal would add that Kali also represents resilience in hostile lands, far from home.

"I'm sorry," I said, "does someone work here?"

"The office is over there." She pointed toward a hall.

The office was easy to find, but it was closed. A sign said it would open at 4pm. I would need to come back after seeing Joanna.

A bulletin board next to the office door was filled with announcements and information about temple activities. I searched through details on upcoming Kali worship times, a schedule for children's classes, a procession coming up in a few weeks, requests for help in the temple, and mathematics and science tutoring. But no mention of the booklet, or even the topic of joyful wisdom. When I turned around, there was another bulletin board on the opposite wall, filled with children's writings and drawings and the words, "What will you be when you are 100 years old?" Almost exactly the same words as in the booklet. This was definitely the right place. I started reading the postings.

> *When I am a hundred, I will be an old lady.*
> *When I am 100, I will set up an old people disco party.*
> *When I am 100 years old, I will still be a singer.*
> *When I am 100, I will lie down on the floor dead.*
> *When I am a hundred, I will dream about 2 hundred.*
> *I will probably be dead.*
> *I will continue to be a doctor.*
> *I will be a pop star.*
> *When I am 100 years old, I will be alive.*

By the time I read the last one, I noticed I had a big smile. I grew up under a very different zeitgeist: finish college, work forty years until retirement at sixty-five, then die not many years later. These kids were growing up free of that worldview.

There was no mention of the class that produced these posts, or the teacher. But I knew I was close.

My phone buzzed. I suddenly remembered Joanna. Sure enough, it was a text message from her, saying she was at the cafe. I fumbled to type an answer as I ran to the street to find a cab. Gibberish came out, made worse through autocorrect. I accidentally pressed send anyway.

A few minutes later, I was in the financial district, walking into a coffee shop at the foot of Joanna's office building.

Joanna was at the back of the cafe with two coffees on the table. She had already ordered me a latte. No teaching, I told myself before sitting down.

"I really liked the thing Misha said at the last Nomads lunch... about her son... asking him for a rating."

I tried to remember what that was. So much was said that day.

"So... I... did what she said... with my daughter."

"What..."

"My daughter is fourteen. She's so... nasty with me. She's always pleasant and laughing with my husband, and she's only mean... with me... when he's not around. So, he doesn't believe there's a problem."

How was I being pulled into these issues with kids? I was never around as a father, always traveling, always busy at the office.

"I decided to ask her what you suggested to Misha. I waited one morning, as she was about to go to school, and asked her for feedback. I told her I wanted to be a better mother."

Oh right, the rating thing.

"She said, you're my mom. I can't rate you as a mother. Then she said, but if you ask me to rate you as a cook, I'd give you a zero." Joanna laughed, then became serious. "After she left, I got angry. Why is my worth as a mother tied to cooking?"

She looked at me as if I might know. I shook my head.

"That was my mother's generation," she continued. "I don't need to cook. We have a live-in helper. At the same time, I can't get rid of the idea that I..." She pinched the tip of her nose, pushing down the emotion. "I tell myself... her meanness is something I am responsible for. She's only mean to me!"

I wanted to touch her hand, resting on the table, to comfort her. I resisted, thinking it was best to let her process her emotions on her own. That's what Misha had said about a client having an emotional moment. Let Joanna learn from herself, let her dig into her own wisdom. Let her teach herself.

"Everyone thinks I'm so strong. My husband... everyone at work. But now..." Her eyes teared up. She shook her head and frowned, as if to push the emotion away. "Now... it's... no... I'm... falling apart."

She sipped her coffee.

"I'm... sorry," I said.

She looked surprised. "It had to come to a head. I've been suppressing this for too long."

She finished her coffee and looked at her phone.

"I need to be back at the office."

I nodded.

She was about to stand up, then settled back in her chair again.

"Tell me how to deal with this," she said.

"Wow, I wish I could. But... I can't... I don't know at all." Then I remembered something Amit said. "Maybe... maybe one thing."

"Tell me. Please."

Just a tiny bit of teaching. I looked over my shoulder, immediately realising there was no way Misha would be listening.

"Can you find a way to be kind to yourself?"

Joanna stared at me, her eyes bigger and even more full.

"You're developing more empathy," I said, "at work with your team... and with your daughter. But can you... start maybe with yourself?"

She sighed and shrugged.

"That would be hard."

"How can you have empathy for others if you're not empathetic to yourself?"

She nodded.

"Well," she said, "I used to practice a meditation called Loving-Kindness. I haven't done it in years."

"That's a great practice."

"You know, I'm going to try it again."

"Your daughter sounds like she's very bright."

She lit up and laughed. "Oh! She is much too bright for me!"

"I remember once, when I was her age, I caught my father with a logic trap that made me feel proud and strong."

"What did you do?"

"Education was always very important to him."

"Like all people from the East."

"Yes, he was like many parents you would know."

She laughed.

"So, one day, I said to him, Dad, education is the most important thing, right? I knew what he would say, and he did... Oh yes, he said, it is absolutely critical; I'm so glad you see that... The trap was so easy to set and he didn't even see it coming. I said, school is more important than anything, again knowing he would agree... Yes, yes, he said, you can't get ahead without an education. And then I said... so then, why is it that when I'm sick, I must stay home from school? Health must be more important than education."

She laughed, "Oh that was mean."

"He was silent. No anger, no shouting, just stunned silence. I walked away, feeling so superior."

"Teenagers are terrible," she said, smiling.

"At the same time, I had so much respect for him. Looking back, I know I also hurt myself by rebelling against what I respected in him."

"I wonder what my daughter is going to remember years from now." She looked at her watch. "I have to get back to my office."

"And I have to go back to the temple in Little India. I'm trying to find the person who wrote this." I showed her *Five Steps To Joyful Wisdom*.

"I've seen that at a sandwich place near here. It's down Amoy Street."

Change of plans, then... I had to get to the sandwich place first.

"Tomorrow is David's son's Bar Mitzvah," she said. "Are you going?"

"Of course! I'll see you there."

The sandwich shop on Amoy Street was a couple blocks from where we were. It looked like a new-age place, with lots of vegan options advertised at the entrance — spinach pesto, Thai peanut, Mediterranean grilled eggplant, and even vegan tuna and Sloppy Joes. Next to the order counter was a small stand with free local newspapers, a few magazines for customers to read, and several copies of *Five Steps To Joyful Wisdom*.

"What would you like?"

"Do you know who put these here?" I picked up one of the booklets and showed it to the man behind the counter.

"They just appeared one day. Just a sec..." He went to the backroom and spoke to someone then came back out. "We'd like to know how to get more. Our customers love them and we're about to run out."

"If you find out who is putting them there, can you call me please?"

He nodded and took my number.

Then, back to the temple. It was almost 5pm, the office would be open.

When I got there, the office door was still locked, with the same sign saying it would open at 4pm. I knocked, but no answer. Maybe they were doing something around the temple. I wandered through the corridor, back into the main area with the black Kali statue, and outside toward the street. There were more people praying now. But nobody doing temple related work, although I realised, I wouldn't know what that might look like.

A man smiled at me; his hands pressed together in a silent Namaste greeting. I nodded back.

"You seem lost," he said.

"I want to speak to someone at the office. But there's nobody there."

"She was here. She just left."

"Will she be back?"

"I don't know."

"Will anyone be back at the office?"

"Try tomorrow."

There was nothing left to do here. I went home and re-read step two of the manuscript, *Seeing Into The Beautiful Abyss Of The Mind*.

While reading it, I found I was more committed than ever to becoming a coach and was excited about pushing through any internal barriers blocking me.

There was another emotion mingled with the excitement. Was it a sense of anticipation at what could be? Yes, but not just that. Anticipation mixed with acceptance that I will keep finding trolls in the beautiful abyss of the mind... and mixed with something else. What was it I sensed? Was it joy? I smiled as I realised this was exactly what the manuscript was trying to teach. I began reading the next chapter. Step three, titled *Detaching From The Illusion Of Self*, was all about learning to let go of old identities blocking us, so we can become who we want to be. It would be very cool to discover how to be more joyful, more of the time.

The Immortal Ones - Part 2

On their way to the waterfall, the couple walked past the neighbour woman sitting on her porch, wrinkled, and hunched over in her chair. They said hello. The woman said nothing. Instead, she tossed a small pebble at them, which they dodged. The old woman had lost her husband years ago, and her children had grown and moved to the mainland. She never spoke. Whenever she ran out of pebbles, she would slowly step into the road to gather them up again. Villagers often brought her food. Children sometimes brought her fresh pebbles from the river.

At the waterfall, they took off their clothes and stepped into the water, laughing, kissing, and splashing each other. After a while, their skin became loose, a layer of very thin cloth, easily removed.

The breeze and the cool water made their fresh skin tingle. It felt like jumping into a fresh-water lake after spending a day in the sea. Waves of shivers started in her groin, bubbled up through her belly and then shot up her spine and exploded in a burst of tingling at the top of her head, causing her to shake with pleasure.

They held their old skins in their hands and said a prayer of gratitude.

"Thank you for protecting me," the old woman recited the words her sister taught her. "Thank you for allowing me to feel the sun, wind, rain, and caress of loved ones. Thank you for hugging me with love and care for so many years."

When they let their skins drift away, carried by the current, the woman's skin became tangled on a branch downstream, where the river was deep and fast.

"It will drift away eventually," her husband said.

Playing in the water, caressing each other, hugging, kissing, and making love, they were like teenagers again, discovering their sensual bodies for the first time. The man gazed at his wife with wide eyes. She could feel his eyes admiring the curves of her breasts, her back, her hips and legs. And the hairline that used to draw him to her neck and ears. She splashed cool water over her body. The tingling sensation was irresistible.

Waves of energy kept creeping up her spine and bursting at the crown of her head.

"Did you feel that?" he said, clearly sensing the same thing.

She nodded.

"It's so delicious," she said.

They laughed walking home, dodging the pebble tossed at them when they were near their place. They stopped to gather up the pebbles in the road for the old woman and placed them in her lap.

When they got home, the woman stopped at the garden to pick plantains to have with dinner. Her husband went on inside. She immediately heard her granddaughter squeal from inside the hut, the sound the child always made when she or her husband came back into the hut.

As the woman chose the ripest plantains, she wondered how her life might change now that she had given up her old skin. Her sister and others had lost friends when they became young again. She worried that might happen to her too.

When the woman stepped into the house, the child was sitting on her grandfather's lap, holding his face and stroking the smooth skin.

"Hello little one," the woman said.

The child's eyes opened wide and stared at the woman.

"It's me, my love," the woman reached out to embrace the little girl.

The girl screamed and burried her head in the man's chest.

It was as if the child didn't recognise her. That didn't make any sense. She recognised her husband; why not her? The woman knelt to the child's level and tried to stroke her hair, causing the little girl to scream and hold the man even tighter.

The woman stepped back. She was scaring the child. She closed herself in the bedroom and sat on her bed, trying to understand. The sobs outside the door stopped. As the woman sat thinking, the emptiness after losing her daughter came back in full strength as if it had happened yesterday. The same sense of extreme loss, guilt, and even worthlessness. These feelings had subsided after she had committed herself to caring for her granddaughter. But now, with her purpose gone again, the feelings flared back up, even stronger.

What will happen if her granddaughter cannot accept her being young? She pulled her knees up close and rocked back and forth on the bed.

The next morning, the woman went back to the river as the sun was rising and found her old skin. She untangled it carefully, put it back on, and returned to the house.

The little girl sat up straight and held her arms out wide when her grandmother was back.

Over the next weeks, the old woman stayed home while her husband worked in the fields. He took up playing drums again, in the evening after the crickets came out. Something he loved doing as a young man. Soon he was playing with friends at a gathering place nearby. The old woman would sit outside the house, listening to their music and laughter in the distance.

Once, she overheard him speaking with her sister, when she was inside, and they were in the garden.

"It's so beautiful to be a beginner again," he said, after trying a new rhythm on his drum. "I am so alive, with so much energy inside me. I can smell and taste so much more! Even the dirt! Such a rich smell I had completely forgotten!"

"I know!" the woman's sister said.

They both laughed.

Later that evening, after her sister left, and her husband was playing his drum, the old woman came out and stood in front of him. She was sleepy and wanted so badly for him to come to bed. But she didn't dare ask.

His eyes opened wide when he saw her. He stopped playing.

"Will you come to bed soon?" she said.

He put away his drum and followed her into the hut.

Later, after he fell asleep, the old woman sat up in bed, holding her knees to her chest. Her throat was dry.

How much longer before he meets a younger woman? He lay next to her snoring. So close, yet so far away.

The next morning, he insisted on washing her hair. He patiently combed out the tangles. Then he cut her nails. He put away his drum all next day and the following day. But he couldn't keep away from it for long though. Soon, he was back out after the sun went down, playing his drum with friends, while she stayed home and held their granddaughter.

Part Three
Detaching from the Illusion of Self

Weapons Of Mass Separation

The elevator to the Synagogue's social hall had no buttons. As I was about to get out and look for the stairs, a woman pushed a stroller into the elevator and blocked the entrance.

"It's a Shabbat elevator, no buttons," she said to me, and then waited.

The doors closed and we went up to the second floor. Moments later I was seated at a table at the front of the room, with David and his closest relatives.

"You must be Jewish," David's father-in-law, Pierre Cohen-Darmont, said to me in French. I was seated next to him at the Bar Mitzvah for David's thirteen-year-old son, Gabriel.

"Are you sure you're not?" David's mother-in-law sounded just as convinced as her husband.

"I probably have Jewish ancestry somewhere." As soon as I said this, words from the manuscript popped into my head.

When we laugh and play
with our many identities...

"I have so many labels, I don't think I can count them," I said.

"Labels are weapons of mass separation," David switched to English, even though his in-laws probably didn't understand. His wife Léa glared at him from across the table.

"Aidan's family comes from Morocco," David switched to French.

"Just my father. My mother is American, Scotch-Irish, going back a couple hundred years."

"But you speak French?"

"I went to French schools from ten to seventeen."

"Tell them where you lived," David said.

"Cairo, Rome, and Paris."

They nodded but looked confused.

"You were born in Morocco?"

"No, the US. I was an expat kid."

"His parents were spies," David winked at his mother-in-law, who didn't seem to know how to take David's statement.

"They were teachers," I laughed. "University professors."

"Just a cover," David said.

"By the time I was twenty-one, I had spent half my life outside the US and already spoke French, and a little bit of Arabic."

"No Hebrew?" Monsieur Cohen-Darmont still looked confused.

I shook my head.

when we see that all of these
are masks...

"You definitely have Jewish blood," his wife said.

I did have many of the labels that made me part of the community they were familiar with. Middle Eastern ancestry... check. French speaking... check. Dark hair and a closely cropped beard like David and many of the other Southern French and North African Jews at the Bar Mitzvah... check.

"What's your family name?" Monsieur Cohen-Darmont was determined to get to the bottom of my story.

"Tell us your mother's maiden name too," David laughed. "How about your first car? And your first pet's name. And the name of your bank!"

"Perez," I said, "and yes, I know, that's a Jewish name, but my father swears his family has always been Christian."

"Of course, you're Jewish!" Mr. Cohen-Darmont exclaimed.

"The man told you he's not Jewish," David said. Then he turned and whispered to me, "But your father maybe didn't know everything about his past."

"I suspect you're right," I whispered back to him.

I wondered if this was why I was seated here while Rajiv, Joanna and Misha were at another table. I wanted to get some time with Rajiv to apologise, but things weren't working out as planned.

"Aidan is a Third Culture Kid," Léa told her parents. "Just like your grandchildren. He grew up in places that were not his parents' countries and spoke languages his parents didn't speak."

when we let go
of outdated labels
even if we still love them
very much...

"TCK is just another label," David said in English. "I hate labels. I hate when people care more about labels than the actual person."

"Wow... nobody talks about your labels more than you do," Léa shot back with a very brief, ice-cold stare. "You collect them like a ten-year-old collects Pokémon cards."

"I don't..."

"HR executive, former Googler, ex PayPal, French, Jewish," Léa's list came out rapid fire.

David frowned at her. I wished I could be at the table with

Misha, Joanna, and Rajiv.

then,
our genuine, authentic, joyful self
can shine through,
more complex,
more beautiful,
than any label
could possibly capture.

Léa's parents looked concerned. They might not have understood the conversation between Léa and David, but the tone was clearly an argument. Mr. Cohen-Darmont swatted at a fly. His wife waved at her grandson standing at another table, beckoning him to come over. Gabriel beamed and immediately came to her.

"Look how grown up you are," the grandmother hugged her Bar Mitzvah grandson. "And so handsome!"

"Merci, Mamie." Gabriel was just as fluent in French as he was in English and, I assumed, Hebrew. I understood his Mandarin was quite good as well. He pulled a chair over to sit next to her.

"Tell me more about this Third Culture Kid thing," Madame Cohen-Darmont said to her grandson.

"That's someone who grew up in a culture different from their parents' culture," Gabriel said. "The third culture is a mixed identity."

"The term didn't exist when I was growing up," I stepped into the conversation. "I just grew up feeling very strange."

She nodded at me.

"I often feel strange too," Gabriel said.

"You shouldn't feel strange," his grandmother said.

Third Culture Kids develop a sense of connection to all of the cultures they've been exposed to, without feeling like they belong to any of them. Their identity is constantly changing, separate from any single culture. It tends to be rooted in people, not places. Home isn't a place; home is a feeling — a sensation of movement, change, transition. It's a strange feeling that's hard to explain to others. Third Culture Kids get along best with other Third Culture Kids, even if the specific mix of cultures is entirely different. They are connected by the common experience of being citizens of everywhere and nowhere. It's not a common mix of cultures that binds them, it's the common experience of being "in-between," not truly belonging here or there.

"I bet most of your friends are like you," I said.

"All of them," Gabriel answered. "Except maybe a couple of my Singaporean friends."

"When I was a little older than you, my last year of high school, I moved back to the US and felt completely out of place. The girls all looked the same with big puffy hairdo's... like Farrah Fawcett."

Gabriel and his grandmother both looked at my oddly, as if they didn't recognize the name.

"She was a famous actress in the seventies," I said.

"I hope I don't feel strange when we move back to France."

"Of course, you won't," Madame Cohen-Darmont said. "I'm sure Monsieur Perez eventually adjusted to his new life."

When I became an adult, all I wanted to do was live in a diverse, multicultural environment. That's where I'm most comfortable. So, I moved to France and built one of the first multilingual and multicultural startups in the country. Today there are lots of them.

"You know," Madame Cohen-Darmont turned to her grandson, "your Mamie is also a Third Culture Kid." She glanced briefly at me, as if to make sure I heard her say the term in English. "I too grew up in a culture that was different from my parents'. They lived in the same country they had grown up in, but it was as if they lived in a foreign land. The culture they grew up in was gone when I was a girl."

I loved her perspective.

"The past is a foreign country; they do things differently there." I tried to remember the name of the novelist who said that.

"Exactement," she looked at me with a glint in her eye.

"Did you know," her husband said after listening in, "the world population has doubled since I was a boy? There are two times more people alive today. That makes a very different world."

Wait... was he my age?!? I often said the same thing about population growth. He had to be fifteen or twenty years older than me. And yet... we were probably born at a similar time, considering how quickly things changed since then.

"Maybe we're all becoming Third Culture Kids," Léa said, definitely looking at least ten or fifteen years older than Val.

"Anybody still living in the past would stand out like a guy in a bar with a moustache and sideburns," I said, "wearing a polyester suit and white shoes with buckles who wants to know your star sign while buying you a drink."

Léa laughed. "My kids have so much in common with children living in China or India playing the same online games and using the same iPads and iPhones."

David was quietly listening. I turned to him.

"Even with all that, I think I might be a bit with you, David. What you said about labels..."

"I hate labels."

"Maybe I think of myself more as NOT something," I said, mirroring the words I had read in the manuscript.

"What do you mean?"

"Not really American, not really French, not Middle Eastern. I don't know if it's a TCK thing or just me. But all my life, I've felt like I'm not this or I'm not that."

"Maybe you're a neti neti," Rajiv's deep voice came from behind me. I hadn't noticed him standing there. "I'm about to leave and I overheard your conversation."

I jumped up, hoping to find a way to persuade him to talk to me a few minutes.

"A Yeti?" Léa looked at him quizzically.

"I've never been called a Yeti before," I laughed.

"Neti neti," Rajiv repeated.

"Not this, not that," I wouldn't have been able to say this without having read the booklet.

"Precisely," Rajiv looked impressed. "It's an ancient negation meditation, to let go of all identities."

"That sounds cool," David said. "I'm sure I have a few labels to get rid of."

Rajiv said goodbye to everyone and turned to go.

"Rajiv, before you go. Can we talk?"

He stopped and looked at me, then nodded the Indian way, wobbling his head side-to-side.

"I only have a couple minutes," he said as I followed him to the door.

"I... I'm really sorry if I... offended you."

He glanced down, then over my shoulder. He hovered as if he was about to duck out the door, then finally looked at me.

"I can't change what happened. People are careless. You can't trust anyone to be one hundred percent careful."

"Yeah, no, I understand. I didn't mean to imply..."

"They do stupid things."

"Accidents happen."

He looked at me with blank eyes, as if I could never understand.

Rajiv's phone rang. He took it out of his pocket and glanced at the screen.

"My taxi is downstairs. I have to go."

I went back to the table and overheard David's father-in-law raising his voice about something.

"Everyone wants to be a coach," he said to David. "All the people who took early retirement are coaches now."

"That's not what I'm doing," David said.

"So, it's a fad here too."

To avoid the conversation, I went to sit with Misha and Joanna.

"How is Matt today?" I asked Misha quietly.

She shook her head. Something was off. This wasn't the best place to talk.

"I saw you with Rajiv," Joanna said.

"I feel bad," I said. "I shouldn't have said what I did the other day, at the restaurant."

"You're fine. He's struggling."

"He seemed depressed," Misha said.

"He did." Joanna nodded.

"You noticed too?"

"Yes, definitely."

"He's in a dark cloud."

As Misha and Joanna continued sharing their perceptions, I glanced over at David still seated at the same table I had been at, and still in a heated discussion with his father-in-law. I hatched a plan to take him out for a drink after the Bar Mitzvah.

"What do you think of that?" Joanna was speaking to me now. I had missed her question.

"Sorry... the noise..."

"I might have a project for you."

"Oh?"

"I told my boss about the orchestra conductor analogy. He loved it."

"Oh! Cool!"

"Yeah, he thought it was perfect for me. And..."

"I'm so glad."

"He encouraged me to get formal coaching. For my team too."

I could do that. Misha was listening. When I looked at her, she nodded at me with her eyebrows raised.

"And I'd love you to do it."

"I would love to."

"I think... the same way I needed to find an analogy... like being an orchestra conductor... I think my team needs the same thing."

"To discover who they are as a team."

"Yeah... that. I need to help them find a purpose, and become more independent, so they can make their own decisions, without me. I've been accused of being a mother hen... I want to stop being that."

Here was proof I could go it alone, without depending on Misha for all of my work. I could bill full price without Misha as an intermediary. Maybe I didn't need to be certified after all. Clearly, Joanna wanted to hire me regardless of certification.

"I've been doing a lot of work with labels recently," I said. "Individual and group identities. It's part of the coach training I'm doing. And..." I was about to mention the booklet, but suddenly wanted to keep the knowledge for myself. "What you're describing sounds exactly like that."

"It would be great to know who we are as a team."

My mind was already visualising a workshop version of the Not This, Not That exercise described in the manuscript. It would be completely corporate focused, without anything that sounded spiritual.

"We can start with a workshop activity that helps your team let go of identity labels that are no longer serving them. After that, we can explore new labels that fit who they want to be next."

"That sounds perfect."

The workshop would just be the start. After building credibility with Joanna and her team, and then her higher ups, eventually, when the time was right, I would re-connect with Vincent Goh and the executive committee. This project, starting with just a single workshop, could develop into something much bigger and set me up in my new career.

After the Bar Mitzvah, I went back to the temple. This time, the office door was open. Inside, it looked more like a large walk-in closet than an office. No windows, a wall packed floor to ceiling with file folders, and a corner filled with cleaning material one would normally see in a janitor's closet. Right next to the door, a young woman sat at a small table, her face lit up by the glow of a laptop.

"Can I help you?" She looked startled to see me.

"Yes, I hope so." I showed her the booklet. "Have you seen this? Is it from your temple?"

She took it from me and glanced at it briefly, then looked up at me and shook her head.

"Have you heard of anything with a similar title?"

"*Five steps to joyful wisdom...* it sounds familiar. We might have had a few of these booklets some time back."

"The book asks that exact question." I pointed at the children's bulletin board on the other side of the hallway. "Who will you be at a hundred."

She bent her head to see outside the door and cocked her head at me. I must have looked strange, a tall white man asking weird questions.

"I'm sorry," I said. "I'm trying to find the writer of this book. Maybe the person who created the bulletin board might know."

"The kids came up with the idea on their own in their Sunday class."

"The kids?"

"I was teaching that day. It was my class."

I must have looked disappointed because she stood up and smiled at me.

"My name is Sheena." She reached her hand out.

"Aidan."

"Wait, let me see that again."

I handed the booklet back to her.

"I have seen it, actually," she said. "At a sandwich place near my office. In the financial district."

"On Amoy Street?"

"That's the one."

"I talked to them. They don't know either."

She was engrossed in the booklet now. She was so interested that I let her keep it. And I left my number, in case she discovered anything about the booklet.

As I was leaving, she called out, "Have you tried Google?"

Obviously, anyone would try searching online.

"Great idea," I said. "I'll have a look."

Detaching From The Illusion Of Self

Un-labeling is the process of letting go of parts of our identity that no longer serve us. The illusion of fixed labels gets in the way of discovering our genuine, authentic self. Our growth becomes blocked. We hold proudly to labels that define us in ways that we like and appreciate, and we avoid the labels that define the parts of us we dislike. In both cases, through pride or avoidance, like or dislike, the tense and rigid grasping hold is the same. Like clenching a flower until it decays in our fist, and still we can't let go of it because we remember how beautiful it was. Authenticity is about seeing beyond the labels. Who am I as an individual, without the labels? Who are we as a team or organization?

Later that afternoon, I met up with David for a walk at the Botanic Gardens. He said he wanted to talk without alcohol in the way.

"Léa wants me to move out," David blurted as we started to walk.

"Oh man, I'm..."

"It's fine. Things haven't been good for a while."

He didn't look fine. His neck was bent over with his chin almost touching his chest.

"When?"

"Soon. I guess."

We walked side by side.

"We haven't told the kids yet. They're not going to take it well."

I was in no place to give relationship advice. That would be like a jungle rooster telling an eagle how to fly. So, I listened silently.

"Our dreams don't overlap anymore. I used to have big dreams. I saw us living all over the world. Then we moved to Singapore and now I don't have the stamina to make another move. I stopped playing my guitar and writing songs."

Lunch at the Bar Mitzvah came to mind. That moment when Léa looked at David and said he collects labels like a ten-year-old collects Pokémon cards. More than her words, it was the look that flashed briefly across her face like a dark cloud on an otherwise sunny day. The curling lip, wrinkled nose and hardened facial expression that lasted a fraction of a second but still sent a recognisable chill along the back of my neck and sinking feeling in my stomach. I knew The Look... it revealed disgust.

"I don't even know what her dreams are anymore," David continued.

"What do you want to do?"

"Just walk."

"I mean..."

"I guess... I... want to... make it work."

Part of me wanted to see David and Léa work out whatever problems they were facing. But my gut was stuck on the dark cloud I had seen across Léa's face. Recovering from The Look felt impossible. The opposite of love isn't *hate*. It's disgust. I knew that more than pretty much anything else I knew.

"I'm trying to become a better person," David said. "Coaching helps. I'm listening better than ever before."

"I love how we're in constant personal development."

"Yeah... all the time."

"When I'm coaching someone," I said, "and I'm in the zone... the sense of being in the present moment is amazing... it's the same as a deep meditation."

"I know that feeling."

"It's... almost... spiritual."

David paused a moment.

"But I'm afraid it's too late," he sighed.

"There's always hope." I struggled to say something to help him feel better.

"I guess..."

"I believe that." Actually, probably not.

"You've been married... you've got some experience in this area."

"I don't know much about... long term... loving relationships." I chose not to add that I did know how to recognize the signs of a failing relationship.

"What happened?"

"Where to start?"

"That bad, huh?"

"You know... I don't really know what happened. It was so long ago. I remember when Val... Valérie, my daughter... was nine or ten... it already felt like the marriage had broken down. I can't really point to one thing. It was gradual. I guess... we just... both stopped feeling needed."

"I can relate to that." He sighed.

"We stayed together another ten years. I was traveling all the time, for work."

"Wow..."

"A decade slipped by," I snapped my fingers, "just like that."

"You stayed for Val."

"Yes, otherwise I would have left long ago."

"That's what's keeping Léa and I together."

"Your kids might be relieved when you tell them. They probably know things aren't great."

"How old was your daughter when you finally got a divorce?"

"We... we never did."

He looked at me.

How much did I want to talk about this? I was over it but didn't want to go into lots of detail.

"She... died... in a car accident."

"Oh! Sorry!"

"Val was nineteen... no, twenty. She was in Singapore when it happened. At the university. I was in London, for work."

"Oh, man... that's tough."

The memory of the phone call was so vivid — seeing an unknown French number on my phone, stepping out of my meeting and answering the call in a wood panelled hallway next to a men's room, hearing an unknown man's voice saying he was with the gendarmerie at Saintes-Maries-de-la-Mer, asking if I was Aidan Perez, and then informing me that Chantal had died in an accident along with another woman in the car. Then later, when I got back to France, seeing the pictures of the accident — a trailer truck carrying iron rods that had broken loose, showering a quiver of iron into the windshield of Chantal's car. The police asked if I knew how to contact the family of the other woman. They had found a Singaporean passport in the woman's purse, but no local contact details other than Chantal's name and address. All I knew was that a colleague from Singapore was visiting Chantal for a project they were working on. It was May 24th, 2005. The day of the annual Gypsy festival. Chantal and her colleague were obviously there to see Sara-la-Kali taken out of the church and paraded through the streets down to the sea.

David and I walked silently through the ginger section of the gardens, with hundreds of species of ginger shaded by high tropical trees and cooled by a waterfall filling the air with spray.

"Hey, what was that meditation you and Rajiv were talking about?"

"Not this, not that?"

"Yes, that one."

"Or not that one," I laughed.

"Do you think it would be good for me to do it?"

"It can help you let go of identity labels that aren't serving you anymore."

"Maybe I'm holding onto labels in my marriage that are messing things up."

I wasn't sure where this was going, but he seemed enthusiastic.

We found a bench under the shade of a rain tree's giant parasol-like canopy. There is an instant peacefulness under a tropical rain tree. The coolness of the shade, and the majestic size of these beautiful trees, always causes me to pause a moment to breathe in fully the experience, as if my chest can expand a little bit more under the protective presence of the dense and high canopy. Sitting on the bench, we began collecting a list of David's labels.

"Husband," he said. "Also, provider, lover, friend..."

"Those are all related to Léa?"

"... and companion."

"Husband, provider, lover, friend, companion," I repeated his list as I typed them into my phone. "What's next?"

"The kids. Father, Dad. Sometimes I introduce myself as a parent, especially at school. Role model, that's a label, right?"

I nodded.

"Can I use adjectives? Nurturing dad, joyful dad, good dad?"

"Sure."

"How about what the kids call me?"

"Like... Dad? We already have that."

"No... Baldy."

I laughed. "Ouch. Mean."

"And Chef. Because I usually make dinner. Pasta Papa! Gabriel used to call me that."

I read out what I had typed into my phone. "Father, dad, parent, role model, nurturing dad, joyful dad, good dad, Baldy..." I had to stop a moment to chuckle. "... Chef, Pasta Papa."

"Yes Man. Add that. Léa calls me Yes Man sometimes, because I don't say no to the kids as often as she thinks I should. And Old Dude, that's the kids again. Add that too."

"How about work?"

"Corporate executive, HR Manager, Boss." He paused as I typed these on my phone. "And a couple different ones. Musician Wannabe. I think Léa might see me like that. And poet. I used to like when she introduced me to her friends as her poet."

I looked through the list again. More than half of the labels were about being a father.

"That's a good list," I said. "Want to add more?"

He thought a moment, then shook his head.

"OK. I'll guide you through the process. Close your eyes... and... notice your breath. Focus on the feeling of air entering and leaving your nose or mouth and filling your lungs."

I closed my eyes and let myself fall into a mindful state as well.

"Notice your body letting go of tension."

I opened my eyes and looked at the list.

"You can open your eyes or keep them closed. Whichever you like."

David opened his eyes.

"Let's start with husband. Say to yourself, or repeat out loud if you prefer... I am not a husband. And when you say husband, make sure you use air quotes."

I watched him say the words in a low, quiet voice.

"Good. Notice how the air quotes soften the statement. When you're ready, repeat the same words again... I am not a husband."

He was quiet now, raising his hands for air quotes as he said the words in his mind.

"If the label takes on subtle, subjective meanings, notice that. The air quotes help your subconscious play with the label. Gently examine the subtle ways in which the label might be limiting you. Simply notice your inner conversation."

We went through each of his words. The ones describing his relationship with Léa, then the ones about his role as a father, and finally the work-related labels. The final label on David's list was poet. When I said, "I'm not a poet," the air quotes brought up a vision of myself at maybe fifteen, playing the guitar. My own assessments of labels like musician and poet had probably caused me to stop playing decades ago. I was a little bit jealous that David had continued.

A pair of Javan Myna birds, distinctive with their yellow-coloured feet that look like fancy sneakers, hopped around on the grass a few feet from the bench. They bobbed their heads from side to side as they looked at us, exploring the possibility we might have some food.

David let out a long sigh, a release of inner tension through his breath.

"Wow. That was intense."

I watched the Myna birds, wondering what kinds of things these life mates might argue about.

"So... much... baggage." David's eyes were red, and a bit misty. "I can't see my identity behind all those labels. I... I lost myself." He closed his eyes again and took a deep breath. "I keep saying I want to be seen by Léa. But I don't even see myself."

"I noticed something interesting," I said. "More than half of the labels you came up with are about your role as a father. Only a quarter of them are about your relationship with Léa."

David looked at me with big eyes, unblinking.

"I'm scared. I'm scared that's all that's keeping us together."

He closed his eyes again. A single, big tear rolled down his face. He opened his eyes.

"I wonder how much Léa has lost her identity, behind all the labels I give her."

David stood up and started walking. I followed him. We walked side by side through the gardens, silently. When we got to the taxi stand, David took the first cab. He turned around just as he was about to leave.

"Hey, I had an idea about your quest." That's what he called my search for the writer of the manuscript — a quest. "I know an AI startup doing text analysis for research. They're a spin-off, from the university. I can ask them to analyse the text."

"Would they do that?"

"Scan it and send it to me."

After David left, I wanted to walk a little more. I didn't have anywhere to be, so I started another round of the gardens.

Joanna called just as I walked away from the taxi stand.

"Quick question... are you a certified coach?"

"Yes... well... not quite yet... soon."

She was silent.

"Hello?"

"So, you're not certified yet?"

"Will that be a problem?"

"My HR head wants me to use another coach... someone certified."

"Ah... I see."

"But I want you to do the training. I looked at the other coach's website. He doesn't have anything near your background."

"I'll be certified soon."

"Anybody can be certified. Real-world business experience makes a difference."

"It's too bad your company doesn't see it like that."

I had twenty-five years of business experience. I had built an international tech company from scratch. I have hired, fired, and mentored people with more experience than probably the vast majority of certified coaches.

"Can you come in tomorrow and meet my HR manager? Maybe you can convince her you're the best choice."

"Text me the time and place. I'll be there."

In that moment, I realised how much I missed the familiar, adrenaline fuelled role of defeating competitors and regaining control of a business opportunity. My brain was already preparing for the meeting, developing a detailed workshop run sheet, reading up on the other coach, and exploring ways to convince Joanna's HR manager. I could call Vincent Goh on the executive committee. We had a very good relationship when he was my client years ago. But that was the nuclear option that would break any potential relationship with the HR manager. I wanted to succeed on my own in this new profession, without depending on old contacts.

Misha might be able to help. She could write a letter stating I would soon be certified. I called her.

"You mean some kind of a pre-certification certificate?"

"Not a certificate. Just a letter."

"You're asking for a pre-certification certificate."

"I guess... when you say it like that..."

"Yeah..."

"The course will be finished in a few weeks," I said. "I'm up to date with everything."

"What if you drop out?"

"That won't happen."

"You haven't been entirely committed. You could still drop out."

I sighed.

"Just convince them with your business experience."

"I'm trying to."

"I can't do it," she said.

When I got back to my apartment building, I almost stopped at Misha's floor out of habit, to pop in and see Matt after school. But things felt awkward with Misha after our phone call. I made dinner by myself and went to sleep early.

The next morning, I decided maybe I was the only one feeling awkward. Misha was always direct with people, so she might not be thinking there was anything awkward about our conversation. Maybe she had even thought about my request overnight and changed her mind. I went down the two flights of stairs and knocked on her door, at our normal time for coffee. Gloria opened the door. Misha was at the kitchen table, and a second cup of coffee had already been set out.

"Is that for me?" I pointed at the extra cup.

Misha nodded. Then she turned toward Matt's room and shouted, "Yo! Matt! Breakfast!"

"I might have been a bit too harsh when you called," she said.

Did she change her mind?

"Not harsh," I smiled, "just direct, maybe."

"Matt! You're going to be late!"

"Does that mean... you changed your mind?"

"Oh, definitely not. But I could have been... less harsh."

Matt came out in his underwear, sniffling, and his eyes red. He wasn't even dressed yet.

"I didn't ask to be born," Matt said. "It's your fault!"

More words tumbled out behind tears and anger, incomprehensible.

"Take a deep breath," Misha said in an amazingly calm voice, "tell me what happened."

It was hard to understand much of what Matt said. Apparently, he had woken up to an email from his father, reneging on his offer. The email said something about not having enough room in the house, a baby coming soon, timing not right... but maybe Matt could come and visit later, in a year or two.

Misha reached out to touch him. He pulled away.

"Matt, listen to me." She emphasized each word. "I. Love. You... More than evolution required. Much more. You're more important to me than anything else in my life."

This made him cry even more. He rubbed his face, spreading tears everywhere, and went back into his room. We could hear him wailing from behind the door.

"Matt!" I stood up and started going to his room.

"Stop!"

"I can help him."

"No!"

"Let me just talk to him."

"Stop trying to fix things!"

"I'm just trying to be helpful."

"Ha! That's BS. You just need to be needed. And there's a great opportunity here with Matt, to scratch that need, indulge that addiction. That's all Matt is to you."

"OK, that's going too far."

"Look... I'm sorry," her voice became calmer, "that wasn't fair. But you need to let this go."

Matt came out dressed for school, his eyes still very red. He had a tissue in his hand.

"You will never lose me," Misha said. "I know you're scared, not angry."

This calmed him. She opened her arms to hug him, but he pushed back at first. She gently insisted, and he let himself fall into her embrace.

Death Throes of a Past Self

Joanna led me past rows of identical grey cubicles to a glass walled conference room. It was just the two of us, at a table that could seat eighteen people. We were waiting for Aileen Wong, Joanna's head of Human Resources.

"Are all of these people in HR?" I glanced toward the rows of cubicles.

Joanna nodded.

"Seems like a lot of people."

Joanna nodded just as an executive looking woman stepped into the conference room, followed by a fifty-something year-old Caucasian man. Aileen Wong took the seat at the head of the conference table while the man sat to her right. He introduced himself as Bill Reynolds, coach, facilitator, HR partner, and another American in Singapore.

"I received your email," Aileen Wong said, "along with your presentation."

"Would you like me to run you through it?" I opened my laptop.

"No need."

That was too fast; her mind seemed to have already been made up. The American stared at me with a smug smile.

"I want to hear more about your background," Aileen said.

As I started going through my bio, a familiar figure appeared at the glass wall, smiling. It was Vincent Goh, impeccably dressed in a designer shirt and pink tie, as always.

"It IS you," he said as he stepped into the conference room.

"I saw on LinkedIn that you knew Vincent," Aileen Wong said, "so I asked him if he'd like to say hello."

I stood up to shake Vincent's hand. Heads bobbed up over cubicle walls, checking out who Vincent was meeting with. The American guy didn't look so smug anymore.

"I know you sold your company," Vincent sat next to me. "Tell me you're only working for pleasure."

"I am," I laughed, "but I still need to make a living. I made some money when I sold the company, but not enough to retire."

"You're too young to retire!"

"And I don't play golf."

Vincent laughed. "You're always doing something new and interesting. What do you have for us this time?"

"I'm an executive coach now."

Vincent glanced at Aileen. "I heard. But what does that mean?"

"He has offered to coach Joanna and her team," Aileen said.

"So... like a regular coach?"

I nodded, instantly feeling like I had fallen down a ladder to a level several floors down.

"Are you combining tech with coaching? That would be innovative!"

"Sometimes... but, no, not really."

"That's right up your alley. Tech, innovation, patents." Then he looked at Joanna. "That's not an area you're involved in, is it?"

"I've asked for help developing my team's leadership skills," Joanna said, "and my own."

Vincent looked back at me, confused, as if he was trying to find some way of connecting his memory of me to what I was doing now.

"I can't imagine you doing anything other than tech. I'm sure our people can learn a lot from your experience as a CEO and an innovator."

I wanted people to get more from me than just that. I wanted to contribute to their lives as human beings, not just as managers.

There was a pause, just awkward enough for Aileen to jump in.

"I agree with Vincent," she said, "you can help our company become innovative and entrepreneurial."

"And lean," Vincent interjected, "like a startup."

Vincent's mobile phone rang, which caused him to rush out of Aileen's office while asking me to stay in touch, grab a coffee, or lunch sometime. The rest of the meeting was a blur. Aileen said she saw me as a domain expert for tech and innovation, with loads of experience. She promised to add me to her list of coaches as soon as I'm certified.

"What about my team?" When Joanna spoke, I realised she had barely said a word.

"You can use Bill Reynolds," Aileen said.

The smug man smiled at her, looking very confident.

"I think," Joanna started, "maybe... we need something a little... different."

Aileen looked at her watch. The meeting was over.

"How about co-facilitating," Joanna said. "Could that work?"

Aileen looked at Joanna, then Bill Reynolds. "What do you think?"

"I love co-facilitating," Bill said. "We can explore that."

My gut told me we would never get along.

"I do occasionally co-facilitate," I said.

"Great. If Bill thinks it will work, I'm all for it." Aileen stood up and left.

"I need to go too," Joanna said.

I was now alone with Bill Reynolds.

"I wanted to meet you personally. We're a big sponsor of this year's resilience and reinvention conference. I saw your name on the list of potential speakers."

"I'm looking forward to the conference."

His mouth curled into an almost imperceptible half-smile.

"Your workshop idea is awesome," he shifted back to today's topic. "Was that your idea?"

I nodded; doubtful he would read something titled *Five Steps To Joyful Wisdom*.

"Have you seen it somewhere else?"

"Nope."

"I am not this, I am not that. Wow."

The whole meeting felt out of control, and I couldn't figure out how to reignite my desire to take control. I couldn't break free of my old self. That was all Vincent and Aileen could see in me. And here I was, being interviewed like someone fresh out of college.

"Let's try it out with Joanna's team," I said.

"Hold on, I'm not convinced they need two facilitators."

"I see."

"It's a small team."

It had been years since I had needed to sell myself. I struggled to keep my shoulders from curling over my chest; there was no way I would let this guy see my humiliation.

"With all due respect," I said, "my approach is fresh, and would be really powerful for Joanna and her team."

He looked at me with a little smile.

"Tell me this," he smacked his lips and paused. "What would you say is the purpose of this intervention?"

"It's what Joanna said. Having her team see who they can be, so they can define their group's purpose."

"That's it?"

"Pretty much, yes."

"That's not what the company wants. I mean... yes, but there's more."

I waited for him to tell me.

"You don't know," he said, "and that's fine. Just say so."

OK, enough. It was clear this was his territory. The markings were clear, I just didn't want to acknowledge it to his face.

Then it got worse.

"Can I give you some feedback?" He looked at me as if he

wasn't used to people saying no. He would give me the feedback anyway. Wrapping advice into feedback was exactly the style of this kind of person. "You need to be fully committed, one hundred percent, with no backdoors, no chicken exit. Do you know that term? It's American."

"I'm American."

"Sorry, I just wasn't sure how American."

Here we go, assessments.

"A hundred percent committed," he continued. "No mentoring or consulting or going back to running a tech company again. You have to get to the point where you have no other choice but success as a coach and a facilitator. Your biggest challenge is going to be unlearning all the bad coaching habits you've picked up."

"Thanks for the feedback."

"My advice, for what it's worth — stay in the tech space, with mentoring and consulting. Why not start another tech company?"

He closed his laptop, ready to end the meeting.

"I have a question," I said. "You're on the selection committee, right? The reinvention conference?"

He nodded.

"I'm looking forward to giving my talk."

Reynolds smiled without looking at me.

"Do you know when the speakers will be confirmed?"

"In a couple weeks."

He was still avoiding eye contact. I was sure he had already made his decision, and I wasn't his choice. That only made me want to do it more. The bigger the challenge, the more worthy the endeavour.

The sensation in that moment was a very familiar one that I hadn't experienced in a long time — adrenaline causing my heart to rush with the excitement of achieving something others didn't think was possible. *Hello adrenaline, my old friend. Partner with me on this; like the old days. I promise there will be a moment when you can express yourself fully, in the most effective way. But right now, just be here with me, and let me admire again your energy — it's been a long time.*

Walking outside after the meeting, I knew I had to break

free of my old self. My past self was preventing me from moving forward. Others, like Vincent Goh and Bill Reynolds, could only see who I used to be, making it more difficult for my new self to emerge. At the same time, it was clear I too was holding on to my old self. A part of me struggled to reach for the future, while another part held onto my past identities — boss, chief decision maker, authority figure. The in-between stage was filled with a sense of helplessness and vulnerability, and I couldn't figure out how to regain control.

Relax and let go. I am not this, I am not that.

The voice in my head reminded me that I hadn't taken the exercise seriously enough. I had helped David work through it and was ready to help Joanna and her team use it. But I hadn't gone deeply into it myself, to truly release my own labels.

I Am Not This, I Am Not That

Can you laugh and play with your many identities? Can you see that all of these are masks? Can you let go of outdated labels even if you still love them very much? That's when your genuine, authentic, joyful self can shine through, more complex, more beautiful, than any label could possibly capture.

The easier labels were at the top of my list, leaving tougher labels at the bottom, like tech founder, CEO and chairman, father, and ex-husband. Instead of starting from the top, which I did last time, I decided to go straight to the labels that were holding me back.

I am not a "tech founder," I am not a "tech founder," I am not a "tech founder."

The declaration, using air quotes exactly as described in the exercise, brought up memories and feelings of loss. The same effect that I had last time I did this.

I am not a "tech CEO," I am not a "tech CEO," I am not a "tech

CEO."

This produced sensations of loss, vulnerability, and loneliness. There was an aching in my chest, and a sense of numbness similar to how it felt when my marriage broke and I finally told my twenty-year-old Val that her mother and I were getting divorced and her response was, "It's about time."

We love holding onto the person we used to be through warm, nostalgic memories, even if they are sometimes painful. The neural ruts are familiar and comfortable. It takes no effort to fall into the well-travelled circuitry. Nostalgia feels good. Jumping out of the ruts takes conscious effort.

Then it hit me. I was experiencing grief. These labels were all dead and gone. I had already come to terms, somewhat, with no longer being that person, although there was still some grief involved. The problem popped into my head with an instant, simple solution — add the word "former" in front of the labels. That was how I actually described myself, a former tech CEO. I hadn't been focusing on the right labels, the ones that were still alive.

I am not a *"FORMER tech founder, CEO and chairman."*

This declaration was scary. It took effort to say these words.

I wasn't a tech CEO anymore... so that would always make me a former tech CEO. That was a permanent label that could never be taken away.

Some of the thoughts and beliefs around your labels might feel fixed and permanent. Pushing too hard to contradict them can be frightening. The air quotes help you playfully approach labels with care and acceptance.

The air quotes softened the declaration and invited me to go deeper.

What would it feel like to not have that title? No more "former tech CEO." What would my professional life be based on if that label disappeared?

My work had drifted far from anything tech related, but the label still gave me credibility... didn't it? Or was it a crutch for my self-worth?

People hired me for my experience... didn't they? What would happen if I removed the label completely from how I described myself? There would be no foundations to build on, just air, and nothing special to stand out from the crowd of other people offering coaching services.

How many years needed to pass by before I could finally let go? Was I becoming like those middle-aged men still talking about their high school sports achievements decades later?

I am not a "tech CEO"... I am just "Aidan."

I was about to force my mind to stay focused and not go down a different rabbit hole, but then decided maybe that's where the exercise would lead to. So, I let my mind wander.

Simply listen to your inner conversation without trying to guide it anywhere. You're not trying to get to a conclusion or reach an objective. Simply become aware of the conversations within you that usually happen at a subconscious level. This awareness loosens up your belief system.

How has my name shaped me? Would I have been a different person if I had had another name? I've often thought life would have been different if I had been named after my mother's side of the family, with a family name more commonly "American." Perhaps I would have stayed in the US, rather than running off to parts of the world filled with people with different sounding names. Maybe I wouldn't have built a company in France that attracted other people like me, with mixed cultural backgrounds. A sense of certainty developed — I would have still found some other excuse to build a nomadic life, regardless of my name.

A memory appeared — in my mid-twenties, in Denver, on a phone call with a computer company for technical support. It must have been 1985 or 1986. Val was a year old at most. The lady on the other end of the line couldn't stop laughing when I said my name. I could still hear her words as she struggled to breathe through her laughter — *I'm sorry, I've never heard a name like that. It sounds like a girl's name.* I needed her technical support, so I waited for her to get over the laughter. Then I started laughing too, trying to make the whole situation light and fun.

Let the visions take you where they want to go. If you can loosen your grip, they will fade away when they're no longer useful. Like waking up to a fresh dusting of snow, covering worn and dirty tracks. You can continue walking along the habitual paths you know well, or you can create new ones in the fresh powder. Instead of holding onto who we used to be, we can become who we want to be.

I am not "Aidan."

Another thought — our egos grow over time in amazingly unique ways. Like a tree adapts to its environment, growing short and tenacious clinging to a rock on a windy mountain top, or, when planted instead in the middle of an open field, expanding its limbs in an expansive way. How differently would my ego have developed had my name been different?

If I am not my name, who am I? If I am not my ego, then what am I?

I am not "my ego."

This wasn't on my list. Another rabbit hole. Obviously, I dive in.

I realised that exploration of labels would at some point lead here. Perhaps this is where the path to wisdom crosses into the spiritual domain of the sage.

All labels are expressions of the ego. They drape the ego like clothing, with different outfits for different occasions and purposes. It's like having access to a massive wardrobe filled with all the fashion accessories one could want. The ego behind all the labels wants one thing — to be different and unique. It wants to stand out, for better or for worse, in a good way or not.

Notice if a label feels like it is drawing out the best in yourself. Is it helping you understand and connect more deeply with others? Is it expansive, opening possibilities? Or does it feel instead like a pigeonhole that restricts you unnecessarily? Has it become a tiny prison of your mind?

Without the ego, we wouldn't be able to distinguish between ourselves and the car coming toward us as we cross the road. When brain scientist Dr. Jill Bolte Tailor had a stroke in her left hemisphere (the part of the brain that says, "I am") her perception of reality deteriorated so profoundly that she couldn't see where her body began and where it ended. The atoms and molecules of her arm blended with the atoms and molecules of the wall she was leaning against as she lost her balance. The ego creates a perception of reality based on the illusion of a distinct individual. An illusion that is both necessary for life, and, as mystics, meditators and sages have known for millennia, is also limiting.

I am not "my ego."

There is a blatant paradox in this statement. "I am" is the ultimate declaration of the ego. So, the statement, I am not my ego, can only be made by the ego.

As I repeated the words several times, I couldn't help but smile. It felt like I was saying something profound, denying the ego, while at the same time I realised the words reinforced the ego's sense of separateness and uniqueness. The sensation was very... human. And funny.

When someone pretends not to have an ego, or suggests their ego has been destroyed, it is clear to most people around them that their ego is making the statement. In this moment, I was playing with what the manuscript called no-self, one of three universal characteristics of existence stating that there is no fixed sense of self because everything is constantly changing.

The cognitive stream of consciousness I was engaged in suddenly shifted to an old joke I heard years ago, an anecdote about the ego that has been told across Central Asia for hundreds of years. A man walked into a village carrying his donkey on his back. The villagers laughed when they saw him, so the man put the donkey down. Once out of the village, he carried the donkey on his back again, so that it wouldn't get too tired. The moral of the story was something like, "Do you want to carry your donkey on your back, or do you want to ride it? It's your choice." The story is part of a large collection of humorous anecdotes and folktales about a wise man named Nasreddin Hodja who often appeared as a trickster, hiding his wisdom behind witty and seemingly nonsensical jokes. Many of the stories include a donkey, which can be seen as an analogy for the ego. Nasreddin Hodja is the Central Asian version of the ancient Greek "scholastikos", a wise man who is so clever that he's stupid. The tales are not unlike Zen koans (What is the sound of one hand clapping?)

Another Nasreddin story — once when Nasreddin was riding his donkey over a hill, the animal suddenly dropped and died. Nasreddin was heartbroken. He dug a grave on top of the hill and buried his beloved donkey. For the next few weeks, Nasreddin cried every day at the grave. Villagers noticed the stranger praying and crying at a new grave and decided a saint must be buried there. After Nasreddin left, they built a dome and a shrine over the grave. Pilgrims began visiting the site, hearing about the unknown saint. Thirty years later, when Nasreddin was back in the same region, he was surprised to find what had happened. "What a coincidence," he said, "my donkey was buried in the exact same place as this holy man."

I am not "my ego."

I'd rather ride my ego than carry it on my back. Can I accept that there are times when my donkey will ride me?

While I can be aware that the sense of separation is an illusion, can I be conscious of its necessity and grateful for the paradox?

Can I also be aware of the ways in which this illusion causes me to judge others and see myself as separate?

Can I see that while I am not any of my labels, I am also all of them and have within me the potential of all other labels?

In the same way that I am not the cells in my body, can I also be distinct from my labels? Every seven years, the story goes, we essentially have a new body. Old cells die, replaced by new cells. The cells lining the stomach are renewed every two days, the cost of being in contact with acid. Skin is replaced every two to three weeks, same as taste buds. We get a new liver every year or so. Fat cells stick around an average of ten years, obviously. Some cells are never replaced, like parts of the brain, tooth enamel and the lenses in our eyes. But the molecules of those cells do get replaced. Molecules throughout the body are constantly being exchanged through metabolism, converting food to energy. If you look at your body right now, what you see was essentially not here a few years ago.

I am not "my body."

Just as waves travel through the ocean, made up of completely different water molecules at every moment in time, our human experience travels through the molecules making up our body, constantly changing and moving, never permanent. We are more like a wave than a table or chair. Yet everything feels so fixed. The changes happen so slowly that we don't notice. Instead, we experience an illusion of fixed permanence.

It's not just cells and molecules that constantly change. Ideas enter the mind, stay a while, then leave. Tastes in music and food evolve over time. Beliefs develop, then fade away. New identities become part of our being, only to be discarded after a while. All of these define us, like the atoms that temporarily make up our body.

If I am not the molecules in my body, what am I?

If I am not the beliefs that become important before fading away, what do I believe?

If I am not the labels and identities that come and go over time, who am I?

When change is slow, these questions are the domain of philosophers. When change is fast, they become critical to everyone.

We mostly acquire our identities accidentally. They develop on their own and get baked into our sense of self through language. The illusion of permanence is strengthened — "That's just how I am." Then, when change occurs, we suffer from holding onto an outgrown identity. The pain is change, inevitable, while the suffering is optional. When an identity is threatened, the brain interprets this as a deadly threat to the self, which it is, because there really is a part of the identity that is dying. The suffering, while optional, can be much greater than the pain itself. The way to reduce the suffering is to become more aware of the identities we adopt.

When I started working, I called myself a Computer Consultant, a C Programmer, and a Relational Database Expert, identifying with several skills that were valuable at that time. A quick search on LinkedIn shows very few people mentioning these skills today. The marketability of a technical skill degrades quickly, so professionals need to constantly upgrade their capabilities. Over the past couple decades, many techies have intuitively learned not to identify too strongly with their skills, to make the inevitability of future change less exhausting. Today, you're more likely to see someone identify themselves as a Software Engineer (a slower changing identity) while listing out various skills that currently happen to be valuable.

Organizations face similar change. Like molecules in the body, the people that make up an organization are constantly renewed. Employees stay an average of four years, while managers, including CEOs, rotate at an average rate of five years. Board members stay an average ten years.

Companies are constantly reorganising. On any given day, organizational changes are happening somewhere in a typical large company. Departments are being merged, broken apart, outsourced, or eliminated.

Think of how many corporate functions have disappeared since the 80s. Secretarial pools, travel planning departments, Quality Assurance (everyone is now a beta tester), Project Management (a role that has become more of a referee in an Agile environment) and middle management in general, along with the associated idea of leadership by job title.

Whole industries have disappeared or are disappearing. Travel agencies, bookstores, video and DVD rental stores, cable companies, and feature phone manufacturers like Nokia, LG, and Sony Ericsson. Companies that identify too tightly with a product category risk disappearing when the product becomes obsolete. Several decades ago, the average lifespan of a large company was sixty years. It's now eighteen.

If our company's corporate identity is not linked to our products and services, who are we?

If our mission and purpose change over time, what do we

actually stand for?

If our business strategy changes with every technological disruption, what kind of company are we?

I was beginning to embrace a mindset shift. From seeking the certainty of solid answers to these questions, to becoming comfortable with staying with unanswered questions for an extended period, perhaps forever. Allowing tentative answers to emerge and disappear with the fluidity of waves across water. Becoming conscious about the use of identity labels. Recognizing their ability to drive us forward in a productive manner, as well as their ability to lock us into tiny boxes and cause suffering when we need to break free.

My biggest realisation snuck up on me. I had been approaching labels though a scarcity mindset since labels take time to cultivate and develop. With more investment in time and effort, they grow more valuable and scarcer. Losing them becomes unthinkable, even if a label has lost its value to others. But in fact, the opposite was true — identity labels are so abundant that we can invent them all the time. Their value is in their temporary nature, like cells and molecules and waves.

The poet Muriel Rukeyzer once wrote, "The universe is made of stories, not atoms."

It was Val who once told me that quote, when she was studying Economics and Creative Writing in Singapore.

She had gone several times to Singapore with her mother, when she was a teenager, and fell in love with the city. When it was time for college, that's where she wanted to go. After the accident, I moved there with her. We rented an apartment together and spent what were probably our best years together. Time went past quickly. After she graduated, Val went on an-around-the-world gap year that eventually took her to Samoa, where she found a job teaching high school French and English. That was a year ago. She has been there ever since.

I am not a "father," I am not a "father," I am not a "father."

I was mostly absent almost all of Val's life. Traveling, working late, even on weekends.

When I was her age now, I never imagined my life would be

filled with so many failures.

Enough of this pity party, I told myself. Enough languishing in these old thoughts. I needed to move. I decided to go for a run at MacRitchie to clear my mind and get back into my body.

The Immortal Ones - Part 3

One morning, the old woman packed her fishing net into a wicker basket, attached it to her back, and took her granddaughter with her to the river. To keep the little girl busy while she fished, the old woman showed her how to find colourful river stones.

She attached one side of her fishing net to the base of a tree and waded through the water to string the net across the river. The water was up to her chest, strong and deep. Her limbs were shaking, frail as a dry old stick that might snap. Her lips and chin trembled. She looked back towards the shore and saw she had drifted downstream. Her granddaughter was still playing with the stones. She turned towards the other shore and pushed herself. When she made it to the other side, she pulled the net tight and attached it to a tree.

She looked back across the river for her granddaughter but couldn't see her. She went to the edge of the water and saw the little girl wandering downstream. The woman rushed along her side of the river, calling, trying to catch the little girl's attention. Sounds of rushing water grew louder. The girl reached for a stone at the water's edge, where the bank dropped off.

"No, baby! Get away from the water!"

The child reached out further and fell into the water. The old woman's heart sunk. The current quickly drew the little girl towards the center of the river.

The woman ripped off her old skin in pieces and jumped into the water with new, youthful vigour, struggling against the rocks, letting the current pull her toward the middle of the river. When she reached her granddaughter, she pulled the girl toward her and managed to get both of them out of the water.

The woman walked home carrying her granddaughter, both shivering. The girl embraced her tightly.

"You're so strong," the woman said, "I'm so happy you're safe."

She hummed a lullaby as she walked home.

When the man saw his wife, young, standing straight and proud, carrying the little girl, he dropped the basket he was repairing and ran to them. He took the child into his arms. The woman felt serene, in charge. She smiled at her husband, as if to say, don't worry.

"I need to go back and finish the ritual," she said.

He nodded.

The woman returned to the river where she had tied the net. She waded across without effort, walked along the river, and found her old skin. She picked up the pieces with respect and gratitude, waded to the middle of the river, and stood in the water, upright and strong, holding the skin to her chest, her eyes closed.

"Thank you for continuing to care for me when I didn't have courage. Thank you for making me safe and comfortable for a little while longer... until I was ready to change."

She looked up into the sky.

"Thank you, my beautiful daughter, for giving me a grand-daughter to care for and love. May you be peaceful. You live in my heart, always."

She reached out and let the skin flow away, watching it disappear into the distance.

The woman gathered up the net and the fish that had gotten entangled, put them in her basket, and returned home.

That night, she dreamt of a cloud on the horizon, in the form of a massive tree, connecting heaven and earth. She sensed the cloud's roots deep in the ground. A merging of earth and sky. A woman in the distance stood facing the cloud tree. Her silhouette was familiar even though she could only see her back. When she was near, she reached out to touch her. The woman turned around to face her. It was her daughter, smiling, her face peaceful, radiant, filled with love. Both women opened their arms and embraced one another.

Part Four
Relinquishing The Lust For Control

Even Goddesses Need Help

There is something magical about waking up to birds singing in a dense city built next to an ancient rainforest. Like most mornings, I woke up noticing the cooing of a zebra dove, the crow of a rooster in the distance, and the distinctive, piercing call — ooh woooo, ooh woooo — of the Koel, an indigenous bird that divides Singaporeans. Some complain about the sound, while others say it reminds them of the small village "kampungs" they grew up in before the city became what it is today.

In the background of early morning rainforest sounds was a vague, almost dreamlike memory. It was something Sheena said when I was at the temple. At first it felt like her words were just a dream, but as I became more awake, the memory became more real.

"Kali is the goddess of radical transformation," I remembered Sheena saying. "She gives us the power to free ourselves from whatever keeps us stuck."

This was what the manuscript was teaching me. There was no mention of Kali, but the transformation Sheena described was exactly what I was experiencing. I was certain there was a connection between the temple and *Five Steps To Joyful Wisdom*. I must have missed something when I visited the temple, so I decided to go back that morning.

When we let go of old dreams

that we still love dearly...

The morning crowd was different. People looked like they were stopping by to pray before rushing to work. I took off my shoes at the door and stepped into the main hall, filled with people.

"Are you waiting for someone again?" The man smiling at me looked vaguely familiar. "It's Amit. From Dabbawalla."

Suddenly I recognised him.

"Amit! Without the hat, I didn't recognise you."

He wore a suit and tie. I had only seen him dressed as a Dabbawalla waiter. The context was so different that he looked like a completely different person.

"So, you found the temple."

"It's hard to miss."

"Sometimes I pray here before going to work."

"Is the restaurant open already?"

"I have an office job too." This explained the suit and tie. Then he nodded toward the black statue. "This temple worships Kali. Other Hindu temples worship Lord Ganesha." He paused, looking at me with a little smile. "They need to address the elephant in the room. We don't."

"Good one," I chuckled.

Amit put his hands together in a silent "Namaste" greeting

and left.

when we celebrate
our successes and failures equally...

Inside the main temple area, I was again drawn to the black statue of Kali. What was I looking for? Without a plan, I wandered aimlessly among devotees praying to the various statues. A woman dressed in formal office wear, an executive in her thirties, prayed to a colourful statue of a motherlier manifestation of Kali. As I was wondering what she might be praying about, the woman looked at me and made direct eye contact before turning and leaving the temple. I decided to go look at the children's bulletin board again, where I found the office door open. The office was empty. But I noticed a small stack of *Five Steps To Joyful Wisdom* on the desk where Sheena had been working. It felt like I shouldn't be here, with nobody around. I turned to leave and saw Sheena.

when we laugh
at the limiting beliefs
that cause us to screw up
magnificently...

"You're back," she said.
"I was hoping to see you."
"Thank you for the booklets." She pointed at the desk. "We saw you dropped them off yesterday."
"It wasn't me."
"Oh? Then who?"
"I have no idea. I'm still looking for the person who wrote it."
She closed the office door and locked it, then started walking toward the entrance.
I have to go to work," she said. "By the way... did anyone from the temple call you?"
"Nobody."

then,

we can live joyfully,
in the present moment,
perform at our
very best,
with our results and our words
in alignment.

"I was about to call and thank you... and then here you are. Also... I showed *5 Steps To Joyful Wisdom* to several others on the committee. They want the writer to give talks on the pamphlet. Like dharma talks." She stepped around several people praying on the floor. "We feel the teachings give a fresh new way of looking at traditional Hindu concepts."

"Great idea. If only we can find the author."

"I have faith you will." She smiled.

"Did you notice how the teachings in the booklet sound very much like Kali?"

"Exactly." Her eyes were big and round.

"Kali represents the part of us that says enough! to our old self... so we can grow and become who we want to be. The booklet is all about that."

"You know Kali well." Sheena looked surprised.

"The idea of transformation and renewal is even more relevant today. Kali was invented in a simpler time." I regretted saying that, since it revealed my own beliefs about deities.

"That's very true. Even Kali has trouble keeping up anymore. Things are changing too fast. She needs our help. Which is why we think the pamphlet is valuable."

"You mean..."

"It's painful and scary to let go of our veils. Instead, we hold even more tightly to when we're comfortable with. Kali helps devotees let go. Your pamphlet helps a much larger number of people let go."

"And they don't need to believe in Kali."

"Today, Kali needs our help."

While I was worried about appearing disrespectful to an ancient Hindu goddess, Sheena's thoughts were even more pragmatic.

"I wonder why the writer didn't put their name on the booklet."

Sheena shrugged.

"What kind of person would print things for free and give them away without getting anything in return?"

"Maybe they want the karma."

"And why sneak around when they could be doing so much good?" I looked up at the ceiling, suddenly having an idea. "Do you have CCTV's?"

"Outside, mainly."

"Nothing at the office?"

She shook her head.

"When did you first notice the booklets?"

"Somebody left them at the office door last night, when I was inside working."

"Maybe we can check the CCTV?"

"There were too many people last night."

"Maybe a janitor noticed something?"

"I don't..."

"What time did this happen?"

"I left just after 7pm. And saw them on the floor, next to the office door."

"Somebody has to know... Surely the CCTV... or a janitor. What time exactly?"

"Stop! I don't know!" She shook her head and continued shaking it silently after speaking.

"I... I'm sorry."

The writer had been so close. Maybe even someone that Sheena bumped into occasionally at the temple.

"Here is what I can do," Sheena said. "I'll put a flyer on the bulletin board with a picture of the pamphlet, asking the writer to come forward so we can schedule talks at the temple."

"That would be great."

"Now, I have to go to my real job. The one that pays my salary."

How I Discovered I Was A Courage Vampire

The final weekend of the coach training program started with an outdoor ropes course designed for team building and leadership development. I had done several ropes courses before and loved the challenge. I didn't know this particular event was about to reveal one of the deepest and most disturbing insights into my leadership style.

We went through the standard orientation. How to put the harness on, how to use the carabiners, the maximum number of people on a platform at any one time (two), and how to back out, if you need to. It was like watching flight attendants going through a safety briefing for the hundredth time.

"You've done this before," the facilitator said to me as she checked my harness.

"Can I go up now?"

"As soon as everyone is harnessed."

Most of the participants were ready, except for one particular woman standing near me, who didn't want to put the harness on. Both Misha and the facilitator were talking to her quietly. I couldn't hear what they were saying, but I noticed she was pale. I had hardly noticed the woman before, since she had been so quiet, and wouldn't know her name if it wasn't on her name tag — Angeline. Eventually, she put on the harness. We went through several basic sections of the course, so everyone could become familiar with the carabiners and all. Then we were ready to go.

When I was at the base of the first platform, ready to start climbing along with several of the more adventurous participants, I glanced over at Angeline, huddled among a group of people. I let people go ahead of me and waited for Angeline.

"Don't worry," I said when she caught up to me. "It's actually pretty easy once you start."

She nodded, unconvinced.

I climbed up the ladder and reached the first platform quickly. Angeline followed close behind. I scrambled across narrow beams to the platform at the other side, trying my best to make it look easy. Angeline followed, with only a brief hesitation in the middle. She smiled at me as soon as she stood on the platform.

After several increasingly high activities, we reached the one that promised to challenge everyone's fear of heights — the Power Pole. This involved jumping from the top of a six-meter-high telephone pole and grabbing a trapeze bar. There were a few nervous laughs as we stood around the pole, most people looking up at how high it was. Hesitating too long only prolonged the fear and would make things more difficult. Which probably explains why I pushed through to the front; somebody had to move quickly and break the group paralysis.

I climbed up the pole quickly, knowing many eyes were on me. When I reached the top, it was difficult to stand up on the tiny round tip of the pole. I crouched a moment, wishing I hadn't gone first, and doubting I'd be able to fully stand. Too many eyes were on me. I stood up. There was clapping from below. The trapeze looked far away, too far to reach by jumping. Moments later, I was holding it, laughing, enjoying the swing of my body, weightless, with the ground far below.

"Let go!"

It took a moment to realise the facilitator was shouting at me. I let go of the trapeze and was lowered to the ground, still laughing.

Others quickly followed. The fear had turned to courage. Even Angeline went up.

After a short break, we went to the final activity of the day. A wobbly bridge six meters high, which we would need to cross in pairs. The facilitator asked us to find a buddy. Before I could choose someone, Misha jumped in and paired me with Angeline.

"You've done this before," Angeline said to me, again a bit pale. Her eyes bulged and didn't blink.

"No need to be scared."

Angeline ran her hand across her harness as she stared up at the bridge.

The facilitator gave each buddy pair an envelope and told us to keep it for later, when we're on the platform. Angeline was still holding her harness tightly, so I took the envelope and put it in my pocket.

Angeline and I were first in line. I climbed up to the ladder, trying my best to boost Angeline's confidence by making it look easy. When we were both on the platform, she held tightly to the post.

"Are you OK?"

She nodded.

"You'll do fine," I said. "It'll be easy."

From this point, I could see that the bridge was made of a series of rickety looking planks with half the planks missing. My legs were long enough to step across the missing planks, but Angeline would need to stretch. It would be best to get across quickly before Angeline became too fixated on the challenge. I was about to clamber across when I heard Misha calling me from the ground.

"Before you start," she shouted, "I want you take out the envelope and open it."

I pulled it out of my pocket and found a blindfold inside.

"There's only one," I shouted back.

"Put it on."

Do we have to do this blindfolded? I glanced at the planks

swaying gently, each plank independent of the others. My throat tightened.

"There's just one blindfold," I shouted louder this time.

Misha nodded at me, her neck strained upward and her hands on her hips. The ropes course specialist standing next to her pretended to put a blindfold over his eyes, and then pointed at me.

"Let Angeline lead you," he shouted.

So, I was supposed to be blindfolded, and Angeline was not. That made no sense. It would be better for Angeline to be blindfolded, so she wouldn't have to look down. I could guide her across easily.

I was about to argue with Misha when I noticed other participants staring up at me. The purpose of this exercise was clearly for me to be blindfolded, making the whole thing more challenging. So, I put the blindfold on. There was some light creeping in the bottom. If I lifted my head, I could see a little bit of the course. To avoid cheating, although nobody would notice, I adjusted the blindfold to be as dark as possible.

"You need to step around me," I said to Angeline, "so you can go first and lead me. Talk to me with every step. Tell me what's coming up next, how wide I need to step over the missing planks. And make sure you're safe first, before you turn and tell me what to do. I'll hold onto the back of your harness so I can feel your movements."

I held her harness, waiting for her to step onto the first plank. But she didn't move. She was shaking.

"Let's go," I said.

She was silent, paralysed.

"Let's go. Come on."

She still didn't move.

I decided to take charge. Still blindfolded, I worked my way around her, back to the front again.

"What are you doing?"

"Follow me," I said. "Hold my shoulders."

Her hands were heavy on my shoulders, and trembling. Angeline was shorter than me, so she was pulling me down.

"Now grab the back of my harness... Yes, like that... hold

tight. Do everything I say."

I was intensely focused on getting across each step without falling. I had to get us both across flawlessly, no trips, no falls, and no awkward struggle to pull ourselves back up. That was my goal. I was fixated on it so hard that I barely heard anything Angeline said, or the voice of the facilitator. And I did manage to get us both across. No falls, no slips. It was flawless. I felt like a hero — powerful, capable, tenacious, all the good sides of stubbornness. I took my blindfold off and looked at Angeline, who smiled back at me with relief.

Then I heard Misha shouting my name from the ground. I looked down to see her waving her arms wildly and kicking sand in the air.

When I got down, Misha was waiting at the base of the ladder.

"What the hell was that?"

"I got us across."

"You don't get it!"

"We..."

"Stop! You don't get it!"

What was she talking about? I got the job done!

"Just... stop... and... listen."

I had never seen Misha furious like this.

"This was supposed to be an exercise for you... especially YOU... to practice giving up control. And trusting your partner." Her voice was quiet now. She pulled me away, where others couldn't hear her easily. "What do you think you did to Angeline?"

I wanted to say that I had gotten her across, but I knew that wasn't the answer she wanted. I shrugged.

"You sucked the courage out of Angeline. And you used it as fuel to drive your need to be a hero."

Ouch. Did I do that?

"You prevented her... now listen deeply... you prevented her from growing and discovering her own courage." She stared at me with wide open eyes and pursed lips, pausing to let her words sink in. "You wasted... WASTED... the opportunity to trust someone else... and learn what it feels like to let go of control."

The tightness in my chest, and the heaviness in my body, told me she was touching on something profound.

"I feel so sad... for both of you... such a valuable opportunity, wasted. Maybe you can see this as a wakeup call... to behave very differently in the future."

Misha stepped away, leaving me alone to stew in my thoughts. She was right.

I felt dizzy, so I sat at a park bench and vaguely watched others going across the bridge in pairs. Several minutes later, I don't know how long, Angeline sat next to me. She put a bottle of cold water on the picnic table in front of me.

"Did you see how many people are falling off the bridge?" She had a big smile. "Dangling in the air like puppets! We just ran across! We aced it!"

"I don't think Misha sees it that way."

"What do you mean?"

"Never mind. You're right. We aced it."

Relinquishing The Lust For Control

Unleashing is about letting go of control. We tend to focus tightly on the goals and dreams that we want, and the path that will lead us to them. We hold them stiffly, making it difficult to see other paths and other alternative goals that might be even more attractive. A tight grip on control makes it harder to adapt to changing circumstances, as we struggle to hold everything together out of fear our world will fall apart. What if I delegate too much and employees make mistakes? What if I hired the wrong people? How can I delegate results and authority if I am not certain I can fully trust someone?

Later at home, while processing what had happened, I went back to *Five Steps To Joyful Wisdom*. The fourth step, on letting go of control, held even more wisdom than I had previously noticed. My initial reading of this chapter had been based on my understanding of delegation and empowerment before the events of the ropes course. Now, a new and deeper reading was possible.

If I were to rate myself on a scale of one to ten, where one corresponds to delegating tasks, and ten means delegating authority, I knew I would generally be around a seven or an eight. I had been satisfied with that level of empowerment, until the ropes course, which suddenly brought the idea alive for me in a way I had never experienced before. I became aware of the pleasure I got from being responsible and courageous, how that made me feel valuable, and how that prevented me from truly empowering others. The awareness caused me to see what was missing to be truly empowering.

I could now see how my courage grows when I support people acting less courageously, prompting me to rise and fill the gap, and, in the process, draining others of their courage, feeding off of them to build my own strength. More like a courage vampire than a leader.

Where I thought I had been helping others find their strength and courage... I was actually using their hesitancy and fear to boost my own courage. The shift inside was visceral. It shattered my self-image as someone who empowers others and builds them up.

I was awakening to the fact that I often put myself in codependent relationships, driven by the belief that I am most valued when needed by others. It wasn't by chance that I was paired up with Angeline. Out of all the people there that day, I chose the one person who would feed my need to be needed.

This was a textbook definition of codependency, a personality style that was first observed in studies on alcoholism. It describes a behaviour sometimes seen in the family and friends of an addict, interfering with recovery through over-helping. If a friend or family member subconsciously identifies with their role as a helper, who would they be if the addict recovered and no longer needed their help? Psychologists have shown how this happens, all subconsciously, until it is brought out through therapy.

How many executives are driven by the need to be needed? People don't generally go out of their way to create an environment that jeopardizes their employees' success and independence — but that's what happens when the need to be needed is more powerful than the desire to empower.

When David asked what happened with my marriage, on our walk in the Botanic Gardens after the Bar Mitzvah, I had lied to him. Well, what I said wasn't totally a lie. I said that we had both stopped feeling needed. But I left out the part about how my need to be needed destroyed the marriage. I could have told him more. I could have told him that I had lost track of what compromise meant and wound up falling into increasingly unhealthy habits. When my wife decided to move to her family's vineyard with our daughter, she casually told me I could come along if I wanted. And so, I followed her, eager to be needed. She complained when my mother and grandmother visited from Colorado, while her mother would visit every day from her home down the street. She wanted to quit working so she could raise our daughter full time, which I agreed to even while trying to build a business. Chasing after being needed didn't lead to love... it resulted in not being needed.

My addiction to being needed didn't stop after she died. It shifted to other people and continued with a string of short-lived dating relationships. I now clearly saw the subconscious belief that had been driving me all these years, the belief that I could only be loved if I constantly provide something valuable to my partner. Earlier in my life, the value was financial. Later, it was more about emotional support. At the end of the day, it didn't matter what it was; I had to be useful in order to be worthy of love.

If I had nothing of value to bring to the relationship, there would be no relationship. If at some point, I could not provide value, the relationship would fall apart.

Looking now at how skilful I had been enlisting Angeline as my partner to make me feel needed on the ropes course, I wondered how many relationships I had unconsciously destroyed, searching for other ways to feel worthy.

The need to be needed had become an unhealthy addiction, an attempt to fill an inner void with external appreciation, stemming from a sense of not being enough. I had equated being loved with being needed.

A question arose — can I be loved without being needed? The question was both liberating and scary.

Relinquishing Expectations

This exercise is designed to help you understand unconscious be-liefs that might be causing you to hold tightly to expectations, both of others and yourself.

What would it feel like to let go of my expectations of others? How about the expectations I had of myself? Could I let go of the expectation that my value came from the knowledge and expertise I could share with others? The expectation that I needed to be needed?

Take a deep breath. Feel the air filling your lungs. As you let your body breathe, notice where you feel the breath. Maybe in your throat. Maybe your nose. Notice your belly, and your chest. Notice how the body presses against your clothes. Notice the weight of your body press-ing down on your chair or cushion.

Now... bring to mind someone you care about.

Val appeared instantly, carrying her overfilled backpack, about to get on the plane, bubbly and excited. I saw her graduat-ing from the university, waving at me from across the room as she laughed with her friends. And I saw her sleeping on the sofa in our apartment in Singapore, looking exactly as vulnerable as she had when she was a little girl.

What would it feel like if you were to let go of all expectations of this person? All expectations, even the smallest ones. How they should act, what they should do, how they should be. What you like about them. What you appreciate about them. Expectations for how they show up, for you. What does it FEEL like if you were to let that go?

What if I dropped the expectation she would come back to Singapore and live here, if not with me then at least nearby? What if she chose not to move to Singapore? What if she moved back to France? What if I could only see her on trips to France? What if she chose not to visit anymore? What if I dropped the expectation that she should call me? But how can I drop that? She should call! I sat with the feeling a moment, letting it settle in. I was overcome by an immediate sense of loss, as if foundations were crumbling into an abyss.

If I let go of my expectations, wouldn't our relationship fall apart? I noticed that having expectations somehow implied that I cared. Can I continue caring without expectations? Wouldn't that lead to not caring? As I sat with these uncomfortable feelings without turning away, the initial fears began to shift.

Other people came to mind — friends, colleagues, clients, my wife.

I realised that when I'm upset with someone (maybe they've let me down or I'm not getting the results I want) I let my expectations drop and the person then becomes less relevant. It's easier to let go by dropping expectations and not caring anymore.

I heard a voice in my head — *If you let go of expectations of someone, how can you trust them?*

It dawned on me. Trust is the expectation that someone will behave a certain way, the way I want.

Trusting that someone will complete their project on time, according to my plan. Trusting they will let me know if they're falling behind schedule. Trusting they will be as diligent as I expect of them.

We trust people who act in the ways we expect, and distrust them if they fail our expectations. So much of what we call trust is actually control. When trust in someone is low, the desire to control them goes up. When you're too controlling, people often believe you don't trust them, and in a way they're right. How to trust someone without being controlling? Is that possible?

The belief underlying my fears was now clear: If I let go of expectations people will underperform and let me down. Seeing it so clearly made it feel less true. What if the opposite were true? Maybe letting go of expectations of another allows them to fly and achieve their dreams. Wasn't that what I had already done with

Val? Isn't that what allowed her to go on the gap year that turned into an indefinite stay abroad? Is it easier to let go of expectations with a child we love deeply?

And then imagine... what if they let go of all expectations of you? What would that FEEL like? What emotions come up for you, when you imagine this person truly relinquishing all expectations of you.

Notice where the emotions lie in your body. Do you feel relief? Do you feel cared for? Unconditionally loved? Or do you feel panicked, clenched maybe? Just notice the emotions.

If I let go of my expectations of someone, they're going to let go of their expectations of me, and then everything completely falls apart. Again, there would no longer be any structure holding the relationship up. How can someone love me if they don't have expectations of me? As I reflected on this, I wondered why, in my mind, love and trust were so dependent on expectations.

A memory flashed of my father's constant expectations of my academic achievements, causing this fourteen or fifteen-year-old-boy to believe that meeting those expectations brought love and acceptance. I realised that my teenage defiance was a way to test those beliefs and see if love was still possible, even if academic results were poor.

What if it's enough to trust that you can deal with whatever happens?

Maybe letting go of expectations allows trust to be simpler, cleaner, without the risk of disappointing. This kind of trust felt safe and secure, not needy and fear based.

With all the uncertainty in our world, how can we possibly continue trusting things will turn out the way we planned? Can I let go of expectations, and trust that I can deal with whatever comes up?

A flash of insight: too much reliance on structure leads to

rigidity, conditional love, and less opportunities for growth and change in others around me.

I thought back to my dream of helping executives in suits and ties cross a busy street in the financial district of a big city. The only expectation was to help people get to the other side of the road. All I had to do was wait for the light to change, then guide a large crowd of executives, all waiting patiently for my signal to walk. They didn't need to be taught how to walk, or how to get to the other side, or where to go or what to do once they were there. My role was simple, and yet profound. Expectations on my behaviour were minor — just lead the way across the street — and yet there was clearly a sense of potential value, perhaps even enlightenment, for people reaching the other side.

A wave of warmth spread through my mid-section, starting in my belly, and spreading to fill my chest with each breath. The possibility of creating loving, caring relationships without expectations felt completely unrealistic, yet amazingly attractive at the same time.

Finally... what would it feel like if you were to let go of all expectations of yourself? No expectations of how you should show up, what you should do. Notice the emotions and the thoughts.

If I let go of all expectations of myself... I would crash on the sofa, stuck in an endless loop of movies and re-runs, and lose all ambition. As soon as this image came up, I knew it wasn't true.

I stayed with the question — what would it feel like to let go of all expectations of myself?

The warmth in my belly now spread to the base of my spine, then worked itself a little further higher with each breath. The tickling in my spine felt peaceful and electric at the same time. After a few breaths, the energy reached the base of my neck, then quickly traveled up my scalp, and exploded at my crown.

I was experiencing what Eastern mystics call a Kundalini Awakening, an explosion of enlightenment as energy blocked at the base of the spine is released. The process has been written about for thousands of years. It is often depicted as a coiled snake located at the base of the spine, which needs to be released through a variety of meditative processes. Many say the process cannot be forced to happen; it tends to occur spontaneously. The neuroscience explanation of mystical experiences seems to have to do with a sudden release of large amounts of the neurotransmitter dopamine. Exactly how that happens isn't clear to me but seems to be understood by neuroscientists. As far as I can tell, questioning deep beliefs — in this case, exploring the possibility that letting go of expectations could lead to greater love and trust, not less — can sometimes cause the brain to re-wire itself instantly, as it shifts from one perspective to its opposite. That's the best explanation I can think of to describe what I experienced.

After it had passed, I didn't feel much different from before, other than a profound sense of peacefulness and optimism, like a low-grade form of euphoria.

The writer of Five Steps came to mind. I had so many expectations of this person, without knowing them. I was imposing my own needs and attempting to control the situation by unmasking the writer, expecting him or her to then produce more writings, mentor me, give talks, teach others. These were all things I would have done if I had written the booklet. In essence, I was expecting the writer to be just like me.

A wave of empathy and warmth washed over me, followed by acceptance of whatever goals and desires the writer had in remaining anonymous.

Whoever wrote the booklet was obviously a wise person. Certainly, wise enough to make their own choices in life. Who was I to expect them to behave differently?

Closing my eyes again, focusing on my breath, counting each exhale, I let my mind settle. After a few minutes, most of the expectations I had examined seemed to have become a bit less fixed. They were still there, but they felt more like sand than concrete. Except one. This letting go of expectations thing was all well and good... but I couldn't stop expecting Val to call. I opened my eyes, took out my phone, and watched Val's video.

"Papa, you're probably sleeping right now, it's very early in Singapore, so I'm sending you a video instead of calling. I'm going to help on the other side of the island, and probably won't have internet for a while. I'm well. I feel useful. Don't worry about me." There was the brief glance away... who was she looking at? "Your birthday is coming soon. I wish I was with you this year." I pressed pause, so I could look more closely at her eyes. Yes, there was pain. Then I realised... she was probably worried about me! I pressed play again. "Papa, there is something I have wanted to tell you. These last four years with you have been wonderful. I'm so glad I convinced you to come with me to Singapore. I will always cherish the time we had together. And... if you're still worried about being away when I was growing up, please stop. You have more than made up for that." She laughed, and then became serious. "And Papa, please remember this... and I hope you hear this... really hear this... the accident would have happened anyway. Even if the car worked perfectly. It wasn't your fault." Then her face became light and smiley again. "Now... I hope the next time we speak; you've found a girlfriend.... finally... and maybe you'll have plans about starting another tech company! J't'aime mon p'tit Papa!" The video ended on her big smile.

From Hero to Sage

My phone rang. It was an unknown number.

"I'm calling about the brochure," a man said, "*Five Steps To Joyful Wisdom.*"

"Yes!" Maybe the poster at the temple worked! "Are you..."

"I got your number from a friend at a cafe."

"Are you the writer?"

There was a pause.

"Sorry... are you the writer?"

"What?"

"The booklet..."

"I run an art space near Arab Street. Could you deliver a few booklets?"

I paused, not sure what to say.

"Hello," said the man.

"Yes..."

"Our members would love them."

"I'm sorry... there's a misunderstanding."

"Your number was at a cafe downtown, in the financial district... next to a stack of the brochure... hold on... Five Steps..."

"To Joyful Wisdom. Yes, I understand. But I don't print the booklets."

"Then... what do you do?"

Great question indeed. I wanted to laugh. What was I doing, chasing after a mysterious writer of an unsigned booklet that was just a few small chapters and a couple dozen pages?

Then the voice: *What if it's enough to trust that you can deal with whatever happens?*

"You know what," I said, "how many do you want?"

"We'd like to buy fifty to start. How much are they?"

I had no idea what the printing costs would be. It couldn't be too expensive, since the writer seemed to be leaving them around town for free. My mind jumped around, frenetically searching for prices of similar booklets, but I couldn't think of any.

"How about five dollars each," thinking about the cost of a latte.

The man paused. Then, "How about a discount for fifty?"

"I'll give you a ten percent discount. Four fifty each piece."

"When can you deliver them?"

"Give me until the end of the week."

The man was silent again.

"If I can get them done earlier, I'll let you know."

"OK great."

After I hung up, I leaned back on my sofa and laughed. I still had no idea what I was doing, but it was fun. I thought about the writer, smiling at me.

Searching online, I found several print shops in China Town. A lady at the first number I called answered in Chinese and didn't want to talk much in English. All she would say was, "Please come to the shop." I called another number that answered in English and gave me more information. They needed a PDF, and I would need to pick out paper sizes, weights, and bindings.

As I scanned the booklet into my computer, I wondered about a copyright notice I might have missed. There was no mention anywhere, so I figured I was fine. If the writer had wanted, the booklet would be copyrighted. Of course, it would then have information on who the copyright belongs to and all that. I told myself I was helping the writer distribute their work anonymously. Clearly, that's what they wanted.

The printer was in a 1980's shopping center next to a food court. The clerk was sitting behind the cash register, eating a bowl of noodles.

"I called around an hour ago about printing this," I put the booklet on the counter.

The clerk put his bowl under the counter and stood up to look at the booklet. After leafing through it, he pulled out a price chart that was actually a three-page document with an amazing number of details I couldn't possibly choose from.

"Can you give me the price to produce exactly this booklet?"

He scratched his cheek and shrugged.

"Why don't you use the same printer as before? Are you unhappy with the printer?"

"I don't know the printer."

"He's my cousin."

"Are you sure?"

"I recognise the paper. And the way he stapled it. See?" He opened the booklet out and flattened it to expose something in the binding that I didn't understand.

"It just looks like a staple, to me."

He shrugged.

The address was another unit in the same building, so I went straight there. If it was the same shop that produced the original booklet, maybe they knew the writer.

Mister Quick Print was tucked between a discount computer store and a traditional Chinese medicine shop. It was the kind of place I walked by without ever noticing.

"Yes, I recognise this," the clerk said.

"Do you print them very often?"

"Mmm... every few weeks. Maybe once a month."

"I'd like a fresh batch."

"How many do you want?"

"Fifty. No wait... a hundred."

"Come back in an hour."

"That's it?"

He nodded. "You can leave your initials."

"AP."

"Those are almost the same initials your colleague uses."

"Do you know his name?"

"Just his initials. AH. It's always the same person. An Indian uncle. Fifty-something. He never leaves his mobile number. Just the initials."

I could feel the writer's presence. He — and I now knew it was a man — comes to this same shop regularly. It didn't feel right though; it felt like I was stalking him, chasing him down even to the print shop he regularly used. I went to the food court for a coffee and a bottle of water, and imagined the writer, AH, an Indian man around my age, in the same place, sitting at the same table, with me, and ordering the same coffee. The man wanted to be anonymous, yet here I was, compulsively chasing him.

An hour later, one hundred booklets were ready. I paid the clerk then had an idea.

"Can I leave a message? For AH?"

"Why don't you message him yourself?"

"It will be a surprise."

The man nodded and gave me a little smile.

That's how I came to leave a message at a tiny print shop in China Town, addressed to someone known only as AH.

I love your work. It has completely reshaped my life.

That was it. No name, and no mobile number. I didn't want AH to feel obligated to call. He wanted to be anonymous? Then I would anonymously tell him I love his work.

When I got home, I laid out the booklets on my dining table. Somehow, I had become AH's helper. I planned on delivering the booklets to the art center the next day.

My phone rang. It was David.

"I have the results."

"What?"

"The AI analysis."

Ah, yes, the text analysis startup.

"The writing isn't ancient," David said. "It's recent. Like in the last ten years. Probably by a woman in her thirties or forties.

Maybe born in India, or in the West of mixed heritage. Spiritual, but not religious. And she has lived in an international environment most of her life. She works in a job that helps people."

"Sounds like it could be anyone."

"Except that this person leads a double life."

"A double life?"

"The analysis says she's attracted to secrets. Her psychometric type makes her suited to be a secret agent. She's comfortable playing with different identities. She could even have a bit of a split personality."

"Could they have made a mistake about the gender?"

"Why?"

"I found someone who has seen him," I said.

"Seen him?"

"The writer. At a print shop. He's fifty-something. And he's Indian. That part of your analysis is spot on."

"Did you get a number?"

"No number."

"I don't have anything more than that."

"This is great. Thanks!"

The Immortal Ones - Part 4

The next evening, the woman took the little girl's hand and walked toward the sound of drums and singing. Her husband and the others were in a circle, playing drums and other instruments while younger women danced in the middle. Her sister was among them. A new couple had joined the group. Foreigners from the mainland, here to bathe in the river, she guessed.

She squeezed herself into an opening in the circle and sat with the others. Drawn into the beat, she clapped along with the others.

When her sister saw her, she stopped dancing and took her hand, pulling her up and inviting her to dance. The woman followed along. Her cheeks ached from smiling. She went into the middle of the circle with her sister. At first, she danced slowly. As if her body needed to get used to the rhythmic movement again. Then faster, her hips shaking. The music picked up a notch, faster drumming, louder. She stamped her feet, spun around in circles, with power and elegance. She sang along with the group.

Mama,
Mama in my heart,
I love you.
Papa,
Papa in my heart,
I love you.
Sister,
Sister in my heart,
I love you.
Daughter,
Daughter in my heart,
I love you.
River,
River in my heart,
I love you.
Earth Mama,
Earth Mama in my heart,
I love you.

The two sisters danced in the circle, touching foreheads whenever they sang the refrain for sisters.

The couple from the mainland clapped and tried to sing along.

"If life were a dream," laughed the foreign man, "what would it mean?"

"Life IS a dream!" a villager shouted. "Isn't it wonderful?"

As the evening was ending, the music died down, and voices turned to whispers, or just plain silence. Couples stared into the fire, arms around each other. Children were beginning to fall asleep. It was time to leave.

The man and the woman walked back home, arm in arm, smiling. The man carried their sleeping granddaughter in his arms. They said hello as they walked past the old woman on her porch, with her pebbles.

The woman stopped.

"I'll be home later," she said.

Her husband looked concerned.

"It's OK," she smiled. "I'll be back soon."

She sat next to the old woman on the porch and spoke of old times, old pains, old losses. She waved her arms as she suggested the old woman could also be young and enjoy the caress of a lover once more.

The wrinkled old woman giggled and blushed.

Part Five
Embracing the Joy of a Lifelong Beginner

Thank You for Being Our Children

Last night, I dreamt about the eagle again. I was in my living room, looking at the wooden deck on the other side of a big sliding glass door. A dark object swooped by. It was the eagle, healthy and strong. The bird landed on the wooden railing, right next to a hummingbird feeder. There, perched on the railing, the big, majestic eagle sipped nectar from a device built for much smaller birds. He was crouched in a bizarre, almost delicate manner, as if trying to make himself small so that he wouldn't break the feeder.

Why was the eagle drinking nectar? Do eagles do that? As soon as I asked this question, I knew that it was the hummingbird nectar that had healed him, the way we know things in dreams.

After a while, the eagle finished. He sat on the railing, looking at the trees.

Suddenly, the eagle turned to me and made eye contact.

Would he try to attack me and crash into the glass door? Would the glass break?

The eagle stared back with a focused but soft look, almost affectionate, his beak slightly open, relaxed. A look of pity, maybe. As if the eagle was saying, "Did you kill my loved ones? If you did, it's just because you're human. That's who you are. You can't help it. I don't blame you for being who you are. But I miss them so much."

I wanted to take a picture with my phone, but the camera app didn't work. When I looked back up from my phone, the eagle was gone.

Laying in that semi-awake state where dream memories gradually fade away if you open your eyes too fast, I found myself reflecting on the meaning of the dream.

The eagle is a powerful, strong hunter, with a sharp and far-reaching vision. This hunter-like persona is what drove me to build a company. For me, these attributes are rarely accompanied by a sense of lightness, and almost never a taste of sweetness. By drinking the nectar of hummingbirds, the eagle must have tapped into their lightness and joy. Perhaps that is what healed him. Perhaps that is what is healing me.

What is the nectar I am drinking? Who are the hummingbirds in my life? The tiny sources of concentrated joy and laughter?

As I lay in my bed reflecting on the dream, Val finally called. I answered and there she was, smiling, happy, excited. As if she had just left yesterday.

"Joyeux anniversaire, Papa!" Her energy poured through the screen, instantly filling the entire room.

"Val!"

"You weren't too worried about me, were you?"

"Of course!"

"I told you I wouldn't have internet."

"It was a long time."

"You worry too much. At least you didn't fly out here to check... wait... did you?"

"No," I laughed.

"I'm sorry." She had that same pout she had as a little girl.

"I was just worried."

"I'm sorry I couldn't call on your birthday. But I got a cake that day!"

"A cake?"

"Not a cake really, a pain au chocolat. It was the closest thing. And I sang you happy birthday. Wait... I'll send you the video."

"Do you have enough clean water?"

"Yes, we do now."

"And how do you sleep?"

"What?"

"Are you afraid of the building falling while you're sleeping?"

"Papa, no!" She laughed. "OK there... you should have the video now."

I watched as she sang happy birthday in French. She even had a candle sticking out of the pain au chocolat. I could feel a smile stretching my face. As I watched, I couldn't help but think I was her age when she was born.

"Thank you, Val," I said at the end of the video.

"Papa, do you remember when we went horse riding the first time in Saintes-Maries-de-la-Mer?"

"You were ten, or nine maybe."

"Definitely ten. It was my last year of Elementary School. It was springtime. I remember clearly. You came home on time to make it to the Gypsy festival with m'man and I."

We had watched the procession carrying Sara-la-Kali into the sea so many times that the memories blended in my mind.

"Do you remember what you said to me?"

I didn't.

"You thanked me for being your daughter."

Her words brought back a vague memory... yes, I might have said that. The conversation might have started with the question she often asked me at the time... "Papa, am I traveler like you?"

"Then, just last year, after the tsunami in Samoa, I wrote this poem for three of my students. Two brothers and a cousin who lived with them. They weren't getting much support dealing with the trauma. They craved connection, but their parents were struggling too... depression... withdrawing from everyone, like so many others. I want to read it to you."

"I want to hear it."

"The poem was written to give the boys a different perspective, the same one you gave me when I was ten. I wanted to help them imagine the voices of all of their parents, grandparents and ancestors... whether they're still here or not."

"Can you read it now?"

She held a piece of paper in front of her and shifted her shoulders, as if getting into a more formal pose.

"This poem was written in the voice of your ancestors," she read, "alive or not... who would say this to you, if they could. It is a celebration of the resilience you were born with."

Then she read the poem in a voice I hadn't really heard before. Melodious, confident, relaxed... yet precise at the same time, stressing the pauses to bring out the poetry.

"Thank you
for being our children,
no matter what age you are.

"Thank you
for gracing our lives
with your imagination,
your curiosity,
your resilience,
and your tireless pursuit
of your dreams.

"Whenever you fall,
you always manage
to get back up.

"You have never
been here
before.

"You don't know
what is coming
next.

"Because you are moving
forward
on your path.

"Thank you
for expanding
our sense of time.

"When we look
through your eyes
and your dreams,
we can sometimes glimpse
the world
decades into the future.

"Thank you
for being our doorway
to discovering
unconditional love.

"When we doubt
our ability to love,
we only need to look
at our feelings
for you.

"In our hearts,
we see you as perfect
in every way.

"Since the day you were born.

"Know
that you are
perfect daughters,
perfect sons,

perfect children.

"You always have been,
and you always will be.

"For being our children,
no matter what age you are,
thank you."

She finished and looked at me with a smile, peaceful like I had rarely seen her.

"Wow," I said.

"Did you like it?"

"I loved it."

"Is that kind of what you were saying? That day? When I was ten?"

"Yes... wow... Wow! That's exactly what I wanted to say."

"I think, if Kali's energy was a real thing, it would bring these feelings out in people."

"That's her fierce motherhood persona."

"After I read it to the boys, they shared it with their friends."

"Do you mind if I share it?"

"I'll send you the text."

"It's so beautiful," I said. "I'm going to send it to Misha. And a few new friends."

"You have new friends?"

"Funny girl! In fact, I'm meeting them for lunch. Guess where?"

"Are you still hanging out at m'man's favorite Indian place?"

"I thought it was your favorite."

"It is. But first it was m'man's. She brought us there, remember?"

Now that she mentioned it, yes, I did remember. It was when Chantal came to Singapore to give her big talk at the university. A colleague had introduced her to Dabbawalla's, then Chantal insisted we go back there.

"You know... I'm giving talks like you now!" Val laughed. "I was asked to read my poem at a community gathering... and then there were several more gatherings and they kept wanting me to read it."

"I'm not surprised."

We talked a few more minutes, then she had to get back to work. After our call, I was surprised at the relief I felt. Life felt light, and wonderful.

A few hours later, I was back at Dabbawalla's for the monthly meeting with The Nomads. Everyone was there, even Rajiv. When we started the check-in process, Joanna went first.

"I asked my daughter for feedback. She's been really difficult with me recently. Typical teenager stuff, but it's gotten nasty. She had a big blow up the other day. I don't know what it was... homework, staying up late on her computer... whatever. I would have normally taken her phone away for twenty-four hours, but I decided to try something different. I asked for feedback... like Aidan suggested at our last meeting. I asked her to rate me as a mother. And she said... You're my mom, I can't rate you as a mother... but if you asked me to rate you as a cook, I'd give you a zero."

Everyone laughed. Joanna smiled.

"At first, I laughed too. Then I got angry, when I was alone. Why did I have to cook? We have a helper! Why did I have to choose between being a mother and a corporate executive? Why? Why did I have to be excellent at both? My husband doesn't have to."

She took a sip of her mango lassi.

"But then something shifted in my mind. One evening, I gave my helper the night off and started preparing dinner. I chose my daughter's favourite dish. Lasagna. She came into the kitchen and said, what are you doing? I'm cooking, I said. She stood around and watched. She didn't help, but we talked. It was the first time in... ages. We talked about memories of our family trip together five years ago."

Amit brought the food and started setting a tray down in front of Joanna, but she didn't notice. She moved suddenly, maybe startled by Amit's presence, and a tray fell to the floor. The little bowls spilled their contents of chickpeas, okra, eggplant, pungent curries, rice and rolled around the floor.

"Damn it, man!" Rajiv jumped up. "Be careful!"

"I am so sorry," Amit crouched to pick up as much as he could. His white Dabbawala hat fell off and landed in the mess.

"It was my fault." Joanna put her hand on Amit's arm.

Amit rushed through the swinging doors into the kitchen and came back moments later with a stack of dish towels.

"What happened next?" Misha asked while Amit cleaned up.

"A couple days later, I found her in the kitchen making a cake. We baked it together. And we talked more. I think she wants to be a cook. And right then... I remembered... when she was little, she used to hang out at my mother's house, watching her cook."

Joanna and Misha stood up while Amit mopped the floor.

"My mother isn't around anymore. This whole thing seems to be about losing her grandmother," Joanna said. "And I never even suspected anything like that."

She sat back down when Amit was done.

"It was so easy to turn everything around," she said. "All I had to do was let go and listen to her. Why did it take me so long?"

"I'd say you turned things around very quickly," Misha said.

"I agree," said David.

"It's good at home, but I'm still struggling at work," Joanna said. "Do I have time to share work stuff? It won't take long."

Everyone nodded.

I loved the blend between personal and work. This wasn't about balance; this was about living everything fully. Not the "having it all trope," but living it all. I wanted this in all of my coaching work. I felt so alive listening to Joanna, even if I wasn't providing any comments, advice, or super thoughtful questions. Just being present, witnessing the unfurling of her thoughts and self-discovery.

"I can't figure out how to stop getting involved in the details. They want me to look over their work. They feel safer knowing I'm there to catch mistakes. I tried asking for feedback, like I did with my daughter, but I didn't learn anything new. Can I get some feedback from you? Misha maybe?"

"You want my feedback?" Misha sat up straight.

"Yes."

"Oh, ok... let's see how to say this... after everything you shared about your teenage daughter, I'm noticing something funny when you switch to work. When I listen to you talk about your team, it sounds like you're talking about your teenage kids. I get confused... is she talking about her kids, or her team?" She laughed.

"Really?" Joanna laughed as well.

"And don't get me wrong. I have a teenager as well, and I see myself doing that."

"I don't know..."

"Does it feel like that? Does it feel like your employees are... teenagers?"

"Now that I think about it that way... yes."

"But they're adults," Misha said. "Not teenagers."

"You're right. I need to keep reminding myself they're adults, not teenagers."

"I'm guilty of that too," Rajiv said. "I just realised it now, listening to you."

"Me too," David said. "And I was just thinking... most CEO's and senior managers tend to have kids still at home, usually teenagers. While board members are often parents of adult children. Their management styles might be reflecting that."

"How about we hear from the only person here with an adult child," Misha looked at me.

"What has changed for me since Val became an adult?"

"And how that impacts your work," David said.

"I think it would be surprising if we didn't bring our parenting styles to work," I said. "I had never thought of it before. When Val was younger, we had rules that looked a lot like KPIs. When she went off to college and I was still supporting her, there were still KPI-like rules, but they were more results based... looking at grades for example, but even those fell apart quickly. Once your kids are grown, the only hope you have of influencing them... is by being inspiring."

"That's what I think," David said. "It would be... a powerful shift... to bring that attitude to leadership."

"To me, coaching is exactly that," I said.

Rajiv wanted to go next.

"When we last met," he said, "you might remember that my commitment to safety wasn't a hundred percent. Nine out of ten, that's what I said. And it's been haunting me ever since." Rajiv looked at me. "I was really angry at you."

He paused for an awkwardly long time, still staring at me. Was I supposed to say something?

"But you're right," Rajiv continued. "What if people are dying because I'm not a hundred percent committed?"

He lowered his gaze and stared at the table. I continued eating, to keep my mouth busy so I wouldn't feel like I had to say anything.

"I struggled with trying to understand what a hundred percent commitment means. It was so much easier to throw my hands up and say ten out of ten is impossible. Then... a couple weeks ago, a janitor slipped and fell as I was walking past. I took off my jacket and put it under the man's head, making him comfortable. And I waited for the medical team. It turned out to be minor. Just a twisted ankle."

He took a sip of water. The others were riveted on Rajiv, barely eating.

"Everything up to this point was pretty normal. It was my nine out of ten behaviour. But then I did something different." His face lit up with excitement as he stared at me and nodded. "I helped the janitor into my car and drove him to his home. His wife was surprised I think to see me. How often does a CEO drive a janitor home?"

He looked at each of us, as if expecting an answer.

"Almost never," Joanna said.

"Never. I stayed with them for a while. Had some tea. And I left when the man promised to take care of himself and recover fully before coming back to work." Rajiv's face broke into a big smile and he slapped my shoulder. "What would you call that?"

"Sounds like ten out of ten commitment," I said.

"Damn right!" Rajiv boomed. "That was my hundred percent. Going just a little further than usual."

Amit came to our table, gathering up trays. Rajiv stopped

speaking. He watched Amit fixedly as if he expected him to make another mess.

"Hey," Rajiv said to Amit, "do you have a twin brother at the Bank of South-East Asia?"

Amit shook his head and fumbled as he tried to carry all the trays at one time.

"I'm sure I saw you there. Can you take off your hat again?"

"Sorry, sir, my hands are full."

Amit disappeared behind the swinging kitchen doors. Rajiv squinted at him as he walked away, then turned back to us and continued sharing.

"I had a brainstorming session with my team about what it means to be a hundred percent committed. Then they had the same conversation with their teams. Culture is shifting. I can feel it."

Another waiter came to wipe off our table and refill water cups.

"We haven't had a single incident in two weeks," Rajiv announced. "No changes in safety procedures, just a different way of being, starting with me." He paused a moment, drumming his fingers on the table. "You know... when I was focused on changing the company... processes, skill sets, employee attitudes... I didn't realise that I was essentially saying... to everyone... hey! You need to change. You! I don't." He turned to me. "I flipped that message on its head. What do I need to change in myself? That's going to be my mantra now."

We were running out of time for any more sharing today, so we decided to wrap up.

"Your waiter friend has an identical twin," Rajiv lingered at his seat. "I saw someone just like him at my bank. Or this guy he has a secret life as a bank executive."

Misha laughed.

"Maybe he's a customer?" I knew he had another job... but bank executive?

"He didn't look like a customer. He looked like an executive. I saw a celebrity couple talking to him in the lobby. And they're definitely customers. He works there, I'm sure." He took out his phone. "What's his name?"

"Amit."

"Let's see," he muttered as he typed, "Amit... at Bank of South-East Asia..."

Then he scrolled up with his thumb, scanning the screen.

"Aha!" Rajiv thrust his phone at me.

I leaned toward the screen and saw a LinkedIn profile with a picture of a professional looking man who did somewhat resemble Amit. Looking more closely, it had to be him. The name on the profile said Amit Hanjabam, Executive Vice President, Bank of South-East Asia.

Rajiv nodded at me, as if to say, see, I was right!

"How admirable," he glanced at the kitchen doors, as if looking for Amit. "Now I feel terrible for losing my temper."

As we were leaving the restaurant, Rajiv asked the cashier if Amit was still around, but he had already left. Rajiv wanted to apologise. I wanted to know if Amit Hanjabam was the mysterious AH. Amit was hiding his job at the bank, so maybe he was hiding a lot more.

Outside on the sidewalk, Misha touched my elbow.

"Can you talk? Just a minute."

"What's up?"

Her head was slightly bowed, and her chin pointed downward. This wasn't the confident and in-control Misha I knew.

"Can... I ask you a favour... for Matt." She looked up at me as if it was very difficult to say whatever she wanted to say.

"Anything. You know that."

"Yes, I do."

"So, what is it?"

"He needs a father figure, as you know. And you're the closest he has."

"I love being that to him."

"It would only be a formality... but... what if you were named his legal guardian."

"Legal guardian?"

"It was his idea, actually."

"You mean..."

"In case something happens to me."

"I..."

"It came out when we were talking yesterday. It turns out he's terrified I may disappear sometime..."

"Absolutely."

"... even if I keep telling him I would never leave him. He said he knows that, but something might still happen to me."

"I would be honoured."

She smiled and squeezed my arm. Were her eyes turning red?

Misha left for a meeting, while I was off to open an account at Amit's bank.

Embracing the Joy of a Lifelong Beginner

Unlearning is about letting go of our authority and expertise. Holding too tightly to what we know prevents us from enjoying the thrill of being a beginner again. Without a shift in mindset, we cannot create anything new, whether artwork, music, a company, or a new career. Fears of letting go get in the way of our creativity. How can I be a beginner without losing my power and authority? How can I manage people that know more than me? What if loss of expertise makes me useless?

The Bank of South-East Asia was in the financial district, around the corner from the coffee shop that distributes *Five Steps To Joyful Wisdom*, and a ten minute bus ride to Dabbawalla. As I stood at the entrance wondering what I was going to do, a young man approached me in a blue polo shirt with the bank's logo.

"How can we help you?"

"I'd like to open an account."

"Of course. Are you a resident?"

"Yes."

"I'll get one of our Customer Representatives to help you."

"Is Amit Hanjabam here?"

"Excuse me? Amit..."

"Hanjabam. I was referred to him by another customer. Rajiv

Murti."

"Rajiv...?"

"Murti. I'd really like to see Amit Hanjabam if I can."

"Let me check. What's your name?"

"Aidan Perez."

The young man walked away and spoke to a woman with glasses and a red scarf, who squinted at me from across the room. The man walked back toward me, under the watchful eye of his colleague.

"We're informing Mister Hanjabam now. You can wait in the Private Banking lounge. Please follow me."

The man led me through to the bank's lounge for major clients, where a hostess offered me a coffee. Moments later, I was sitting in a plush armchair with a coffee, a glass of water and a couple biscuits. As I waited, I pulled up Amit's profile on LinkedIn and read through it again. He had been with the Bank of South-East Asia for over ten years, rising from a middle management position to his current role reporting to the CEO. Before that, he had worked at Citibank and State Bank of India. His profile was filled with endorsements. Clearly, he was well-known and appreciated. Why in the world was he serving tables at an Indian restaurant?

Twenty minutes went by, and I had finished my coffee and the glass of water. I didn't expect to drop by and find Amit immediately free to chat. But... well... I did have my hopes up. The hostess refilled my glass.

"Are you sure you want to wait? Would you prefer scheduling an appointment?"

I looked at my watch, mainly to show I was busy too.

"I'll wait."

After all, I didn't need to be anywhere else.

Another ten minutes went past. Maybe I should have scheduled an appointment.

Then, there he was — Amit, dressed as a senior executive, in a suit and tie, like the morning I saw him at the temple. He stood in front of my chair, smiling sheepishly.

"You found me."

At first I thought he said, you caught me.

"Amit." I smiled back at him.

"You don't really want to open an account, do you?"

"Not really."

"I didn't think so. Let's go for a walk."

He took my empty coffee cup and water glass, waiting on me here just as he would at the restaurant. This time, I felt embarrassed.

*When we let go of
our expertise and authority,*

We walked to a little garden a block away, a lush, peaceful oasis in the shade of tall buildings, with the sound of a waterfall somewhere in the corner, flowing into shallow ponds with koi fish. An elderly couple sat on a bench, watching a two or three-year-old child. Amit went straight to a bench at the opposite end. I wondered if he spent much time here.

"So now you know my secret."

"I have so many questions."

"Why do I do it?"

"Yes, to start. You don't mind if I ask, do you?"

"Every once in a while, somebody finds out."

A woman walked by quickly, in business attire and high heels. Amit was silent as she walked past.

"My assistant knows. And two other people at the bank. They cover for me in case something comes up while I'm out for lunch. I don't want lots of people to know." He winked at me.

Two teenage boys went past, bouncing a basketball.

"What do you call a Hindu god playing basketball?" Amit had that glint in his eye that announced a joke. "Swishnu."

He couldn't help giggle. I laughed too.

"So... why do I do it? That's what you want to know?"

I nodded.

*when we pretend to be
junior apprentices again,*

"I work as a waiter several times a week during the lunch rush, for free. It's a form of service. It keeps me humble. People don't see me as a bank executive. They just see a waiter if they see me at all."

He paused to look right and left and craned his neck to see beyond me.

"When I'm a waiter, customers don't really see me. My ego screams in frustration. I do this work to see my ego try to make sense of not being seen. When I watch my ego struggle, I develop compassion. I can see how this ego is what keeps us alive... the need to be seen and valued as independent, unique beings... and I can see that is entirely what the ego's purpose is."

He paused, looking at me.

"It sounds like a spiritual practice," I said.

"You could call it that. You know, you're very easy to talk to."

"Your story is amazing to listen to."

when we allow ourselves
to act like children
in spite of years of
experience,

"When I'm a waiter, watching my ego struggle in frustration, I am in fact witnessing the power of aliveness within me. In a way that encourages humility."

Amit described several basic meditation practices he enjoyed, all from the booklet. After several minutes, he still hadn't mentioned *Five Steps To Joyful Wisdom*. Then he looked at his watch and stood up.

"I need to get back to the office."

"Can I ask you one more thing? Are you AH? Did you write this?" I pulled the booklet out of my bag and handed it to him.

"What is this?" He took it from me as if he hadn't seen it before.

"It was at your restaurant."

"I don't know anything about it." He handed it back to me.

"I just want to meet the writer."

"I need to go." He turned to leave.

"I just want..."

"I can't help you," he said over his shoulder.

"Do you know who wrote it?"

He stopped, then turned around to face me.

"I can't help you... she's no longer here."

"What?"

Amit darted toward the street.

She's no longer here? Where was she? I went for a walk, trying to make sense of everything. What was Amit hiding? The writer was a woman, just like David's AI startup friends said... and Amit knew who she was!

After going around the block, I was back at the garden again... and there was Amit, sitting at the same bench again, his shoulders slouched, and his chin almost touching his chest. I sat next to him.

> *then,*
> *we can enjoy the thrill*
> *of being a beginner,*
> *embark on new journeys,*
> *and fulfill our purpose*
> *of bringing new creations*
> *into the world.*

"My wife wrote the book." He spoke quietly, staring at the ground. "*Five Steps To Joyful Wisdom*... based on the three universal characteristics of existence... impermanence... suffering... and no-self. That was Kashvi's work."

Then he was silent. The waterfall made its burbling sound as it flowed into the pond. The breeze rustled through the trees.

"She had been working on it for a couple years, before she died." Amit's voice cracked briefly. "Kashvi was close to finishing it. She was already planning ways to distribute the booklet. She insisted it had to be anonymous, through coffee shops and restaurants."

"Why?"

"It sounds kind of silly now." He shrugged. "So specific and detailed. She wanted people to stumble on the booklet. She used to say... serendipity is the heart's way of finding what the mind doesn't know it wants."

"I like that."

Amit nodded and smiled briefly.

"She always loved surprising people," he said. "She liked leaving secret, surprise notes around the house for me to find. She would put notes into my bag when I travelled for work. She would leave invisible messages on the steamed-up bathroom mirror, for me to find when I showered. She loved leaving surprise gifts for friends, or greeting cards, in random places, like on an office chair, or secretly placed in a friend's bag." He giggled now. "Kashvi was always celebrating completely random, unexpected things."

"Why anonymous?"

"It had to be."

I looked at him, searching for more.

"She wanted to shed her persona. She wanted the work to speak for itself... without being interpreted through who she was. She wanted it to be read for itself... not as the product of a hiring executive with a Hindu background."

"She sounds like you."

He looked at me.

"It sounds like the same reason you work at the restaurant, anonymously."

He nodded.

"She was always doing volunteer work. Soup kitchens... restaurants... working as a cook, a waiter, or a dishwasher. But she never wanted friends or colleagues to know. She wanted me to go with her, but I never did... I was too busy... always too busy."

He paused again, staring at a pair of doves that had landed nearby, cooing, and strutting around each other.

"You're married," he said, "I remember you speaking about your daughter. I hope you're a better husband than I was."

"I was married."

"Ah." He was silent a moment, then cleared his throat, causing the doves to fly away. "We spent many evenings imagining unknown people stumbling on the book... becoming intrigued... then finding their lives transformed. All through serendipity. Sometimes I made up names, silly names, of imaginary people who had stumbled on the book that hadn't even been printed yet. I think that made it almost as pleasurable as actually seeing real people discover the actual book."

"You do know it had a big impact on my life. I'm one of those random strangers."

"She saw her book as an attempt to transform Kali's energy into a nectar adapted for today's tastes."

"Nectar? Is that what you said?"

"Nectar... a bit sweeter than how people traditionally see Kali, less bitter, yet packing a surprisingly powerful punch."

"She really called it nectar?"

"The sweet nectar of Kali's transformative energy."

The coincidence triggered goosebumps at the back of my neck.

"That's not in the book," I said.

"After she was gone, I cleaned up the manuscript and created a printable booklet. Then I started distributing it. The first time I put the booklets in a cafe, I could sense her presence so strongly. I was filled with gratitude... and relief... and joy! So much joy! Especially when I saw a random stranger pick it up and reading. I get a big warm heart now when I think about it."

"Was that when you started working at the restaurant?"

He nodded.

"Working at the restaurant and distributing her book... that's your way of honouring her."

"I suppose so."

"I wish I had met her."

"She would have liked you."

"I was wondering... why paper?"

"Paper?"

"Yeah, why not a PDF, or an eBook?"

"Electronic... definitely not."

"Why?"

"She created a work of art. I don't want to change it. That

would feel like cheating on her, betraying her."

"You wouldn't need to change anything... a PDF and eBook will let lots more people read it."

"Where does it stop? Maybe people want a new edition, or revisions... what if the text starts to get changed? Who would change it? What if people want a sequel! Who would write that? It's a slippery slope."

"I agree people will want more. I want more."

"And what about serendipity? People will search for it online. They won't stumble on it like a paper book in a coffee shop."

"I stumble on things online all the time. I buy too much stuff online." I laughed, but Amit didn't.

"Absolutely not! I'm not going to betray her!"

"Lots of people will want to read more from her. I want to read anything your wife has written."

"She wasn't looking for fame. That's not why she wrote it."

"How about talks?"

"Talks?"

"Talks and workshops based on her five-step framework."

"Oh, I get it." His eyes grew larger. "You want to give talks and distribute the book electronically to reach more people and commercialise her work."

I looked at him silently, not wanting to confirm. But talks were already lined up. I had to get him to say yes.

He shook his head.

"Think about..."

"No... definitely not."

"People are probably already sharing it electronically. They can use their phones to PDF the book."

He sighed.

"Think about it," I said. "People read the book, like me. Their lives are transformed. Like mine. Are they going to talk about the book? Quote from it? Share their insights? Of course, they will. I'm sure they already are."

Amit wasn't budging. His arms were crossed tightly against his chest.

"I mentioned earlier that I used to be married," I said, hoping

I wasn't making a big mistake. "We didn't get divorced. She... she died. So, I too lost my wife."

Saying those words felt strange. Who loses their wife? It wasn't like we were out on a walk one day and she wandered away when I wasn't paying attention and I lost her.

He tilted his head toward me, his eyebrows raised.

"It was an accident," I said. "She died instantly."

How much should I tell him? He was silent, his eyes trained on the ground in front of the bench, and his head bent toward me so he could hear clearly.

"Chantal... that was her name... Chantal was driving the car."

"Chantal?"

"Five years ago. A stupid accident. Bad brakes."

Amit's eyes bulged. He slowly raised his hand to his mouth, staring at me with wide eyes.

"My wife also died five years ago. May 24th, 2005."

My stomach clenched. How did he know that was the date Chantal died?

"It was in France," he continued, "a small village in the South, with a very long name I can't pronounce."

"Who are you?"

"You said Chantal."

I stood up, shaking, wanting to get away from whatever complicated con this man had put together.

"My wife died with her. In the same car." Amit's eyes were red, and his voice was breaking. "They were friends."

"May 24th, 2005?"

He nodded.

"Saintes-Maries-de-la-Mer?"

"That's it. I could never pronounce it."

I sat back down. My mind felt numb, paralysed, incapable of making sense. I felt lightheaded, as if I had stood up too quickly and could easily pass out.

"Your wife..." I started.

"Kashvi."

"... Kashvi... was visiting... my wife?"

Amit nodded.

"She was the colleague from Singapore?"

"They weren't really colleagues. Chantal... was helping Kashvi with the book."

"The book?"

He leaned back on the bench, looking up at the sky.

"Five steps... to joyful wisdom."

"This one?" I took it out of my bag. "Are you sure?"

He nodded.

"My wife? Chantal? She worked on the book I've been chasing?"

"Yes, she was helping Kashvi."

"How? Why?"

"They met when Chantal gave a talk about Kali..."

"The talk at the University of Singapore."

"After that, Kashvi asked Chantal for help on her manuscript. She wanted to translate ancient wisdom around Kali into something that resonates better today."

"Wow."

Amit nodded. He put his head back on the bench, stared up at the sky, and let out a big sigh.

"You know, the book looked familiar as soon as I saw it at the restaurant."

Amit glanced at me.

"I might have seen the cover page at home."

He nodded.

"I was so oblivious... I never knew what was going on at home. I was only focused on my work."

"I know how that is."

I leaned my head back as well, feeling nauseous now.

"What a strange coincidence," I muttered.

"I would love to call it a coincidence," Amit said, "or better yet, serendipity. But I'm afraid it wasn't. The restaurant was Kashvi's favorite. She brought Chantal there several times. I joined them for lunch once. Yes... I met your wife."

Chantal must have taken Val and I to the restaurant after she discovered it with Kashvi. My ears were ringing. The traffic sounds seemed far away, and muffled.

Doves cooed nearby, but I couldn't be bothered to turn my head to see them. A bird circled in the sky, high above.

"They died instantly," Amit said. "That's what a man from the embassy told me."

I nodded.

"I dreamt for weeks that I was there when it happened," Amit continued, "looking down from a few meters above the car, in a disconnected way, like watching a YouTube video of a freak event happening to total strangers."

I had similar nightmares.

"And here we are," I said, "five years later."

"I'm happy we met."

I looked at him. Amit beamed. He truly seemed happy.

"Serendipity," I said. "How did that go?"

He looked puzzled.

"Serendipity," I hoped I wouldn't mess up her words, "is the heart's way of finding... what the mind..."

"... doesn't know it wants," Amit nodded, smiling.

It was hard to wrap my brain around the thought that Chantal had been involved with the book. That was why so much of it felt familiar.

"The immortal ones," I said out loud, suddenly making the connection.

"What?"

"The legend in the book. The immortal ones. It's a retelling of an old legend, adapted to my wife's life."

Amit looked confused.

"Chantal's mother died soon after she was born," I said. "And she was raised by her grandmother. It all makes so much sense."

Chantal's grandmother used to say, "Ma p'tite puce, je vis grâce à toi. Tu me rajeunis." Or: My little darling, I live because of you; you keep me young. Her grandparents both lived long, active lives, just a few kilometres away from our home. Chantal's grandfather died just after turning ninety-four, and her grandmother died the next winter, at ninety-eight. The modified legend must have been Chantal's way of connecting with her grandmother.

The connection in that moment was so intimate that I felt like my heart was melting, like butter in the sun, as the French would say. I had been attracted to the restaurant my wife loved, and stumbled on her work there, which resonated because I heard her voice, without realizing it. And then I had felt compelled, driven, to chase down the writer, not realizing that I was actually chasing after my wife's memory.

May You Dance in the Sky

Matt heard from a friend at school that someone saw the eagle a couple days ago. He insisted all three of us walk to the hill looking out over the forest and the eagle nest, to see if it was back. I didn't tell him I had dreams about the eagle again. Misha made him carry a backpack with a picnic blanket and some snacks. It looked like they were ready for a stakeout.

Misha and I walked together while Matt walked twenty or thirty meters ahead of us, as he usually did.

"So, you've been chasing after your wife all this time?"

"More like her ghost."

"Wow. That's... pretty cool."

"Pathetic, yeah."

"No, really."

"I was so distant. For so many years. I never knew what she was working on."

"The book connected with you deeply, because you knew her thoughts so well."

"I guess."

"You said it yourself — the book felt very familiar. You've

been chasing after her memory."

"But... what's hard, is... I don't know... I keep asking myself, why didn't I realise all this when she was alive?"

My heart again felt too big.

"I wish," she said, slowly, as if carefully choosing her words, "I wish a man loved me like that."

"I was never home! We were about to get divorced!"

We arrived at the lookout point. I took the blanket out while Matt studied the treetops with his binoculars.

After a couple minutes, I noticed a large bird circling in the sky. I tapped Matt's shoulder and pointed at the sky. He trained his binoculars on the bird, and immediately burst into a big smile.

"That's him! That's HIM! He's alive!" Then he looked over the binoculars at me. "Aidan! He's alive!"

Matt's hands trembled with excitement. Misha and I both laughed with relief. Until that moment, I hadn't realised how tense I had been as we came up the hill, fearful Matt would have a breakdown if he didn't see the eagle. Now all was good.

We watched it together as it circled the sky, taking turns with the binoculars. After a few minutes, it disappeared over the horizon. Matt sat on the blanket with us and opened a pack of potato chips.

"He'll be back," Matt said. "He's probably just hunting."

"The eagle could probably tell an amazing story," Misha said.

"We can make it up," I said. They both looked at me, waiting to hear more. "We can take turns creating a short story about the eagle."

"Boring," Matt said.

"Great idea," said Misha.

"I'll start the story, then we each take turns seeing where the story leads to."

Matt shrugged. It might have been a boring idea, but he was intrigued. I was sure he was.

"Here it goes... Once upon a time, there was an eagle. A male. He had lost his family. And he was almost gone too. He hid in a pile of wet leaves and wanted to be left alone. The eagle had given up. A man started poking him with a stick."

"That's your dream," Matt said. "I don't have any dreams about the eagle."

"Just make something up."

"Let me think."

"Not too long," Misha said. "See where your imagination takes you."

"OK, the eagle felt the man poking him with a stick. Now the eagle would have to look for a quiet place in the forest to die. He didn't want to move. He just wanted to be left alone. Your turn, Mom."

"I'm not playing," Misha said.

"Aw come on!"

"Maybe after a couple rounds. Aidan, you go."

"OK... Hummingbirds fluttered nearby," I said.

"Hummingbirds?" Matt smiled.

I nodded and continued. "They laughed and argued with each other, darting about. Dancing even. Too much joy in such a tiny package, thought the eagle. The hummingbirds called him to follow them into the forest, away from the man. The eagle crawled out of the pile of leaves and flew with them." I looked at Matt.

"Is that another dream?"

"Um..."

"It is!" Misha laughed.

"Why can't I have dreams like that?"

"Make something up," I said. "Get your imagination going. You'll remember lots of dreams."

"Once in the air," Matt said, "the breeze lifted him above the trees. The eagle skimmed the treetops with his claws, struggling not to crash, because he was very weak. Your turn Mom... just make something up."

"Oh, all right," she said, "The eagle circled the area, searching for the hummingbirds. He couldn't stay up long. He was tired and still sick. That's it.

"Aidan's turn," Matt said.

"He found the hummingbirds darting around a tree, drinking nectar. The eagle instinctively wanted to protect them and feed them, as if they were his eaglets. He was the one who needed care though. The hummingbirds seemed to know that. They darted back and forth between the eagle and nectar filled flowers, encouraging him to eat."

"Eating nectar?" Matt had a big smile. "The eagle tried to sip the nectar, but the flowers broke apart when he inserted his beak." He pointed at Misha.

"The thick sweet smell inside almost turned him off, but his hunger drove him to keep trying."

"Finally," I said, "when it was clear his beak was too big for any flower, the hummingbirds called him to another place, at the back of the man's house. There, on a wooden balcony, they hovered around a feeder, showing him how to drink. The eagle crouched on the wooden railing, trying to make himself as small as possible, and poked his beak inside the tiny feeder. He drank the sweet nectar, surrounded by hummingbirds." I looked at Matt.

"The nectar gave the eagle a burst of energy. He was able to fly straight again, with lightness."

"His provider instincts kicked in," Misha was enjoying this now, "driving him high into the sky, looking for prey."

"Aidan's turn."

"He managed to catch a rabbit," I played along with Misha's theme, "and brought it back to the hummingbirds."

"The eagle tore pieces of meat from the carcass and held them in his beak." Matt clearly liked the gory stuff best. "The hummingbirds weren't interested. He tried waving the meat in front of them, but they ignored the food. Your turn, Mom."

"If he couldn't provide for them, what was his purpose?" Misha looked at me and winked. "How was he to honour his paternal instincts if they didn't need him?"

"If he can't hunt and provide for others," I added to her clear allusion to me, "why would they want him? Why continue living? Death is what happens when eagles can no longer give. This in-between thing was worse than death."

"This is kind of weird now," Matt said. "The eagle gave up trying to feed the hummingbirds. He gradually healed. The eagle spent so much time around the hummingbirds, and drinking nectar, that he started flying like them. He would hover in one place, like a hummingbird, then dart away at high speeds. Just for fun."

"He danced in the sky," Misha said, "unlike any eagle."

It was my turn again.

"Once, when he had done this particularly well, he let out a piercing cry, a long, loud screech. The hummingbirds all fell silent. As did the rest of the forest."

"That's enough now. I'm done." Matt peered through the binoculars toward the eagle's nest.

Misha kept going.

"By drinking the nectar of the hummingbirds, the eagle was able to tap into their laughter and joy. He learned to receive their care and simply offer his presence, without needing to actually do anything other than be there with his friends."

"He was appreciated simply for being who he was," I said.

"Stop now, guys," Matt was focused on whatever he was looking at through the binoculars. "There's another eagle."

I looked out in the general direction he was scanning. There was another bird in the distance.

"I think I see it too."

"Where?" Misha came next to me to see where I was looking. "Oh, there. It's circling. They're both circling."

"With lightness in your being," I said, "and the wind under your wings, oh what sights you must see."

"It's a female," Matt announced. "They're checking each other out."

We watched as the two eagles circled each other from a distance.

The eagles gradually circled closer together. Then suddenly one of them swooped toward the other. There was a flurry of wings flapping as the two birds began falling together.

"Their talons are locked," Matt said. "Definitely a mating ritual."

The birds cartwheeled in the sky, falling quickly. At the last moment, they disengaged and soared back up into the air. Then they did it again.

Matt put his binoculars down and looked at us with a funny smile.

"I think we're going to see new eaglets soon," he said.

"May your wings carry you high, and may you dance in the sky." I say to the eagles — or to myself, I can't tell.

As we walk back toward the parking lot and drop-off point, Matt was especially close to me. At one moment, he put his hand on my shoulder while walking side by side, the way I sometimes saw him walking with Misha.

"I told my friends at school," he said.

"About what?"

"That you're my godfather."

"OK," I nodded, wondering what brought up that conversation. The afternoon sunlight shimmered through the trees, making the path look sparkly.

"Should I call you godfather?"

"That sounds like a crime boss," I laughed.

A familiar sense of being valued and needed washed through me. It felt like it was coming from Matt's hand resting on my shoulder, but I knew it was a cocktail of neurotransmitters coming from my brain.

"God-dad?" He laughed. "Stepdad?"

I wondered if he was hoping Misha and I would get together.

"I'm not really your stepdad, though."

"No, you and Mom aren't married."

"How about just Aidan?"

"Yeah, nuh... that's kind of boring."

"Well, thanks!" I laughed.

If the mix of brain chemicals flowing through me were on a bar's drink menu, it would be called something like Old Fashioned Worthiness — a shot of dopamine for the thrill of being liked, oxytocin for the physical contact of Matt's hand, and several shots of serotonin for the sense of recognition I craved so much. Identifying the emotions and their brain chemicals helped to disengage myself from the addiction. I decided immediately to put an elastic around my wrist that I could snap whenever I felt the urge to be needed.

"We can get more creative," I said. "How about Baba? That's Middle Eastern."

"Like baba ghanouj?" Misha said, walking a couple steps behind us.

I laughed.

"Wait," Matt said, "what does Val call you?"

"Papa."

"When she calls you," Misha said.

"Ouch."

"Just kidding."

Matt walked quietly, clearly lost in thought, his hand still on my shoulder.

"I guess Aidan works best," he declared. "And with my friends, I'll still call you my godfather."

"That sounds like a good plan," I said.

Something caught his attention up ahead. He ran a few steps, then stopped and peered through the thick jungle, holding up a hand toward us, motioning for us to stop and be silent. Moments later, a monitor lizard slithered across the path, its snake-like tongue flicking at the air, tasting for signs of food or a mate.

"An eagle drinking nectar," Misha said. "That's pretty funny."

"It was a dream."

"Doesn't Val have a hummingbird tattoo?"

"I... yes... she does."

Misha nodded.

"She got that after her mother died," I said. "Chantal didn't have a tattoo but said that if she ever got one, it would be a hummingbird."

We walked silently for a few steps.

"The hummingbirds in your life healed you with their nectar," Misha announced, as if that was the true and final analysis.

When we were waiting for a cab, Misha turned to me.

"We're going dancing tonight. You can't say no."

"OK," I said, surprising myself.

She nodded at me, not looking surprised at all.

The Resilience and Reinvention Conference

I sat in the front row next to Amit, waiting my turn to speak, regretting my decision not to bring slides. The longer I waited, the more I wanted to abandon my planned talk and deliver a conventional presentation instead, the kind everyone here expected. But without slides, I was locked into my initial plan. Or was I? Couldn't I just talk about the five steps and what I learned these past months?

The speaker on stage pointed at brain scan data flashing across the screen while talking — lecturing, to be more accurate — about the impact of mindfulness on long term meditators. Off to the right of the stage, standing discretely behind the curtain, was my friend, Vincent Goh, the conference's main sponsor and moderator of this afternoon's session.

"He was on Oprah," Amit whispered while looking down at the conference brochure in his lap. "A neuroscientist who became a Buddhist monk then mindfulness teacher... no wonder he's famous!"

I glanced at the brochure, following Amit's index finger. The title of the session was, 'Exploring the intersection of wisdom, technology, and neuroscience? My session's title was right underneath, and now sounded very silly: 'From hero to sage... leadership skills for an age of uncertainty.' Amit liked the title of my talk. It had piqued his curiosity and reduced his resistance. He wanted to see how I wove in the five steps process, and how I would stay true to his wife's message without mentioning her.

In a few moments, I would be lecturing too, but without the academic pedigree or monastic experience of the man currently on stage. And without slides. I glanced over my shoulder at the audience behind me. The room was filled with executives, businesspeople, a few startup founders, and lots of CEO's — some current and many future ones. In other words, people like me. My story wasn't as colorful as the neuroscientist/monk/Oprah guest speaker, but it was my own story, and I was sure it would resonate with the audience. I could skip the very unconventional introduction I had planned, and just jump into my story. But I knew that would be bland. I felt the adrenaline causing my heart to beat faster and tightening up the back of my throat. Hello adrenaline my old friend. My talk was about uncertainty — what better way to start it than through a moment of uncertainty and discomfort, maybe even a bit of embarrassment, for myself and the audience.

The neuroscientist-monk-meditation teacher finished his talk with a thank you and a bizarre bow. At the first sign of applause, Vincent Goh stepped out from behind the curtain and kicked off the Q&A session.

Someone in the audience raised his hand. A conference aide ran to him with a microphone. The man tapped the mic a couple times, then spoke.

"We tried a mindfulness program for our customer service staff, and it backfired. It made them more depressed. You see, they have to put on a fake smile dealing with obnoxious customers, which is easier if you're daydreaming about your next vacation instead of being in the present, miserable moment. Performance crashed and our staff turnover rate went through the roof!"

"So..." Vincent stammered, "I'm sorry... so was that a question?"

"No, I just wanted to share my experience."

Vincent nodded at him.

A woman raised her hand.

"We did something similar. Mindfulness did work with our tech developers. We got a productivity boost without increasing payroll. And it was a huge hit with senior executives. We just have to be careful and deliberate about how we use these tools."

"Thank you," Vincent nodded at her.

A woman at the back stood up with a microphone.

"What would you say to someone who complains that mindfulness is just a new management tool to increase productivity and get more out of employees?"

"Great question," the Monk said, clearly pausing to get his thoughts together. "Mindfulness is about being fully present and aware in the moment. It's the opposite of multitasking. So yes, it leads to increased productivity, but also better health, satisfaction, and relationships with others."

"A win-win," Vincent said.

Several hands went up in the audience.

"Let's move on, now," Vincent said, ushering the Monk off the stage to a round of applause. "Our next speaker has been on several panels with me, in other conferences. I have known him for almost a decade and consider him a friend. Many of you know Aidan Perez as a tech entrepreneur. His life has been one of constant transformation. His most recent transformation was from hero to sage, the title of his talk. He is here to share his secrets with you."

Vincent retreated to his spot at the edge of the stage, behind the curtain, as I walked on stage. Here we go.

I stood in the middle of the stage, looking out at the audience as the applause died down. There is almost never silence after the applause. Speakers usually talk instantly, filling in the silence with as many words as possible to fill in their allotted time. When the speaking doesn't happen, a sense of awkwardness quickly descends on the entire room, as it did now.

My gaze rested somewhere at the back of the room, a simple way to avoid eye contact with the audience as I settled into a period of unannounced, unscripted, and immensely awkward silence, other than the ringing in my ears. In the first moments, I imagined people thinking something was wrong. Maybe I had forgotten my speech. Maybe there was an audiovisual problem and music was supposed to be playing. After a few moments, it would become clear the silence was purposeful.

Rather than focus on the ringing in my ears, I focused on my breath, using it to anchor me. The in-breath tickled the back of my nose and caused my chest to rise. It felt like I couldn't get enough air into my lungs.

I accidentally caught the glance of a woman in the audience staring at me with her jaw open and a puzzled look. I closed my eyes to focus on my breath and ignore the intense desire to speak and break the silence.

The ringing pounded in my ears.

The slightest sounds became welcome interruptions.

A paper ruffling.

The air conditioning system droning.

Voices talking and laughing somewhere outside the room. Traffic on the road... a truck going by, a car honking.

A cough from the back of the room, followed by another cough up front.

And then the murmuring began, coming from different parts of the room in waves.

Somebody stood up and grumbled as they stepped past others and made their way to the doors at the back.

More mumbles and whispering and louder grumbling.

And still, I let the silence continue.

The sounds gradually died down.

I let my eyes take in the audience. Some people had their eyes closed, with small smiles, possibly meditating in the unexpected silence. Others looked at their phones, blue screen glow lighting their faces.

A man giggled in a middle row, then burst into laughter, triggering more giggles and laughter. I let a small smile come across my face and allowed myself to make eye contact with someone laughing. I closed my eyes to let the moment pass. The giggling gradually faded away and the room was silent again. I took a deep breath and let it out with relief.

"You lose your grip," I said, "and then you slip into the Masterpiece. That's one of my favourite quotes from Leonard Cohen."

The silent room stared fixedly at me. Maybe Leonard Cohen wasn't their generation.

"Younger people here would know his song, Hallelujah, which has become a very popular ballad."

I took another deep breath and slowly exhaled.

"You lose your grip, and then you slip into the Masterpiece. Did you notice that happening? Moments ago, when things didn't unfold as expected, when there was silence instead of a Power-Point presentation. What did you experience in that moment? Perhaps at first you were surprised. And then felt awkward... like I did. Perhaps there was judgment... what in the hell is he doing just standing there? I paid good money... just to see this?"

There was laughter, and I laughed too.

"Or you might have appreciated the silence and fallen into a light meditation, while at the same time wondering what was happening. Whatever you experienced, however way you responded to what was happening, I would say that was a reflection of how you might respond to uncertainty and events happening outside your control."

I took a deep breath again, then repeated the quote, "You lose your grip, and then you slip into the Masterpiece."

As I scanned the room, I noticed Vincent sitting in the front row, near the stairs leading to the stage. He smiled at me. I nodded back at him. Then I turned back to face the room again.

"Did you feel your grip? Did you notice the grasping? The desire for certainty and control? And then, after a little while, did you feel the letting go?"

There was lots of nodding in the audience. A man had a big smile. I pointed at him, "You get it, don't you? You felt the letting go. That right there is the natural quality of resilience we all have. That quality of losing our grip and slipping into the Masterpiece."

Then I described the five steps to personal and organisational transformation.

First, choosing to enter the path of transformation, having a deep desire to change. Starting from the top of the organization, where the intention to change begins before rippling out.

Second, learning to embrace the paradoxes that multiply in the deep abyss of our minds. Not only embracing, but actually developing a love for the paradox and cognitive dissonance that are part and parcel of the way our minds work, and the way our organizations function. Loving being human. Recognizing and acknowledging the creative ways we avoid taking responsibility and ownership of the events that happen in our lives, as individuals and as groups. As all human beings tend to do. And then making new choices, responsible ones... as all human beings tend to do.

Third, detaching from the illusion of self. Learning to let go of the labels and masks that limit our fullest potential. I shared the exercise — I am not this, I am not that, giving the audience a taste of my own unlimited set of labels. Applied to the organization, the exercise becomes, "We are not this, we are not that," opening possibilities for new ways to see ourselves and our products, services, customers, and stakeholders.

Fourth, relinquishing the lust for control, a key trait of leaders who empower and inspire others. I shared my ropes course story, where I learned to loosen my grip so others can be heroes.

Fifth, embracing the joy of a lifelong beginner, an ongoing practice of letting go of expertise and authority and being a beginner again.

Here I shared my two eagle dreams, bookending the start and culmination of my latest transformation. From the eagle languishing under wet leaves, dying, to the same eagle healed by drinking hummingbird nectar. I explained how I saw the eagle as the part of us that is a powerful, strong hunter, with a sharp and far-reaching vision. In my case, this instinct is rarely accompanied by a sense of lightness, and almost never a taste of sweetness. I have always been far more comfortable hunting and providing for others, than receiving. By drinking the sweet nectar of hummingbirds, the eagle in my dream taps into their laughter and joy. He releases past failures, guilt and shame. He finds healing and recovers the ability to dream.

"Who are the hummingbirds in your life?" I asked the audience. "You know, the ones who want to give to you without receiving anything in exchange. Imagine how pleased they would be if you were to let them bring sweetness into your life. Imagine where your life might go next, free of guilt, shame or whatever it is you want to let go of. With lightness in your step, and the wind under your wings, oh what sights you must see. May your wings carry you high, and may you dance in the sky."

And I was done. I bowed my head toward the audience. Vincent swept across the stage clapping his hands with a mic tucked under his arm.

"Before we open the Q and A session," Vincent said, "there is just something I need to say. Hallelujah... Leonard Cohen's song... it's become popular during the Christmas season... but it's about a Jewish man's lust for a beautiful woman bathing naked."

"A surprising theme around Christmas," I smiled.

"That's a paradox, right? That's the kind of paradox you're referring to."

"A cultural paradox," I nodded.

"And for me, personally," he paused, holding his elbows tight at his sides, "that song has always represented something I have grappled with in leadership... and in life too, actually."

He took a deep breath. As if he wasn't sure he should say more. I nodded at him and waited for him to speak. The silence in the room was gorgeous.

"There's a continuum in this song... good and saintly, versus flawed and human. I see these continuums everywhere, with different labels. Like at work, mission versus people. The desired state... versus human reality. And because it's a continuum, from one side mission... and the other end of the continuum people... I never know where to be on that scale. I feel that same struggle in Leonard Cohen's song."

He paused again, looking at me with his mouth open, as if he was searching for words.

"What I heard in your talk was something new... maybe there is no continuum. I think that's what you're saying. At least it's kind of what I heard."

I nodded. "That's beautiful. Yes, what if there is no continuum? What if everything is good and saintly and flawed and human? What if our work is all mission and all people? That's a powerful insight."

"Now I'm wondering," he said, "how has my belief in this continuum impacted my company? The culture of my team. How has it impacted the people around me?"

I could see the impact on Joanna, who believed she could be demanding or supportive, not both.

"Letting go of that belief might open up lots of things for you," I said. "I'm so pleased you got something of value from my talk."

I glanced at Amit, hoping he would be hearing all this. Amit nodded at me.

"Let's open the floor to questions from the audience," Vincent said. "I see someone ready with the mic." Vincent pointed at a man standing at the side of the room.

"You talked about being all mission and all people," said the man. "What are other examples of a paradox?"

Vincent nodded, looking at me.

"Wow," I said, "let's see. There are probably an infinite number of variations. We're very creative like that. Here are a few I've heard recently. Leaders can be demanding or trusted, not both. You can focus on your work, or your life, but work-life balance is mostly impossible. I have to delegate and give my subordinates more autonomy, but any mistake they make would cause me to look bad. If I let go of control, how in the world would anything get done?"

"I have one," Vincent said. "I have to propose ways to increase profits while benefiting the communities we operate in. But at the end of the day, shareholders only really care about the stock price."

"That's a common one," I laughed.

"Or... I have to drive innovation to compete, but our legacy systems take up all our resources and slow us down, in comparison to startups without all that baggage."

"Did we answer your question?" I looked at the man in the audience.

"I recognize so many of those," he said. "I hate them, but is it really possible to get rid of character defects like these?"

"Oh gosh, I don't see them as defects. I see them as cracks giving you a peek into your wisdom. They only become apparent in areas that are important for you. Otherwise, if it's not something important, you won't even notice the paradox. They appear when your mind is trying to reconcile your inability to achieve something that is important. It's a self-protection mechanism to explain away difficulties. Like... I can't really have great results and a happy and engaged team, so it's OK if I just choose one of the two. The magic is that now you know this is an area that's important for you. The crack shows you that. So, you can then play around with replacing the or in your belief statement with an and. Who would I become if I were to believe that it's possible to have great results AND a happy and engaged team? I don't know, maybe an inspiring, engaging, and empowering leader."

A couple more questions and I was done. I sat back down next to Amit.

"I like how you've embodied Kashvi's five steps," he smiled at me. "You've made them your own."

"So, are we good?"

"We're good."

Locked Talons

The vibrant music from the live band pulsed through the thick tropical air, causing my shirt to vibrate to the Latin beat. I had never been to Havana, but imagined the tropical climate was very similar to Singapore's, creating an authentic feeling at the Mojito Bar. As my eyes adjusted, I noticed the musicians were a mix of Filipino and Malay, while the lead singer was most likely Hispanic. My kind of melting pot.

The dancers were an even larger mix of people. I noticed a tall, Caucasian woman dancing in the middle with an even taller Indian-looking man. Their spins and turns were dizzying. The woman's red dress swished as she twirled, while her partner elegantly glided around her, creating a space for the woman to express herself as passionately as she liked. What was most striking was the big smile on the woman's face.

"If there was a Little Havana in Singapore," Misha said, "it's heart would be right here."

I touched my chest.

"The music is too loud," I said. "I can feel my shirt vibrating."

"You're weird," Misha laughed. Then she turned to face me with a smile. "Aidan, are you about to dance?"

My shoulders were moving to the beat, and my hips too, maybe. I shrugged. It was hard not to move.

"I can't dance. When I try to, I look like I'm walking through a giant cobweb."

She laughed.

"I don't think I'll stay long," I said.

"I know, I know."

"It's way too loud here."

"Early to bed, early to rise... what the hell is wrong with you?"

The tall woman in the red dress was dancing with another partner now. I wondered how many of these couples were actually together.

"That's Kate," Misha waved at the woman in the red dress. "She's beautiful, isn't she?"

I nodded, sipping my beer.

"I tried to set you up with her."

"Oh?"

"You weren't interested."

Someone dropped a beer bottle near me, shattering and splattering several customers. The air became thick with the smell of beer. An employee appeared seconds later with a mop, motioning for me to move. I backed away and bumped into someone. When I turned around, it was the tall woman in the red dress, dancing with her partner.

"Sorry!" She shouted at me with a big smile, then salsa'd a little further away.

"My fault," I muttered, knowing she couldn't hear me.

Where was Misha? She was next to me moments ago, before the bottle broke. Then I saw her on the dance floor, with the tall Indian man.

The sound from the band was too loud and wouldn't let up. When the trumpet was especially aggressive and insistent, the drums would jump in and try to be even more imposing. Each musician seemed to be competing to be louder and more energetic than the others. There was hardly a pause between songs — didn't they need a break? I didn't think I could last long in the bar, what with all the noise, mixed with the thick smell of alcohol, beer and sweat.

Coming here tonight was a mistake. But I couldn't just walk out, without saying bye to Misha. So I finished my bottle and ordered another one. Two guys next to me were doing tequila shots, thumping their glasses down on the counter after each one, and now they had a bowl of nachos. I was tempted to order nachos too, but I wasn't going to stay long enough to eat them.

The singer spoke in Spanish, breaking out of his singing voice, announcing something to a room full of people who for the most part probably didn't understand a word he was saying.

Misha came over and grabbed my arm.

"I don't want to dance," I said.

"We're moving to a table."

She pushed through the crowd, pulling me behind her. Suddenly we were standing at a round bar table next to the tall woman in the red dress.

"It's much better here," Misha said. "I ordered nachos."

Misha introduced us.

"Get to know him quickly," Misha said to the woman, "he might turn into a pumpkin soon."

I learned the woman's name was Kate O'Brien, a high school principal at one of the international schools in Singapore — I couldn't hear which one — originally from New Zealand, who loved dancing Salsa and Bachata.

"So, you're not with any of the men here," I pointed toward the tall Indian man.

"Just me, all by myself. Divorced, no kids. And I try not to date other salsa dancers, anymore."

She and Misha laughed, then clinked their glasses. Clearly a salsa world inside joke.

"Misha told me you've been here a few years."

I wondered how much more Misha had said.

"Almost five years now."

"Where will you go next?"

"My daughter's grown. She's in Samoa. I'm free to go anywhere, but for now, Singapore is home."

"It's a good place."

I nodded. The band's lead singer started a new song, suddenly filling the bar with music. I realised I hadn't heard them for a while. They had taken a break while we were talking, and I hadn't noticed.

"Shall we go out to talk?"

"No," she said, "let's dance."

She was already walking toward the dance floor, moving her hips to the beat. She turned around and smiled at me, motioning for me to follow her.

"I can't dance," I shouted over the sound of the music, "no rhythm."

"Nonsense. Just move with me."

It was very hard, but I wanted to dance with her. She was patient and seemed to enjoy showing me how to move. It was all pleasure to her. We danced several songs together, and I think I eventually could hear the four beats she kept repeating — ONE, two, three four... ONE, two, three, four...

This woman didn't need me. She was strong and independent and in charge of her life, I was certain of that. And yet, I was attracted to her. I liked that she didn't need me. I liked even more that I was attracted to her anyway, without needing to be needed. A new thought came to my mind — did I need her? Was I attracted to her because I needed her in some way? I glanced at her shoulders whenever I could, half expecting to see a hummingbird tattoo. But there were no tattoos, as far as I could see.

When we finally stopped dancing and she went to the washroom, I was alone with Misha.

"You like her."

"She's.... pretty cool."

"No, you like her. I can tell."

"Yeah, maybe I should have listened to you."

"About?"

"Setting me up."

Misha broke into a huge smile.

"You're circling each other on the dance floor," she said.

"Please don't lock talons right here in front of everyone."

"Your mind is messed up. Really messed up."

"Save the locked talons thing for later," she said with a straight face.

And then I burst out laughing, a deep, belly laugh, with tears and all.

"Locked talons," I sputtered. "You're so bizarre!"

Misha pressed her forehead against mine, and we both laughed.